Foreword by
**Chef Harpal Singh Sokhi**

Design & Illustrations by
**Abha Baxi**

Photography & Styling by
**Niranjan Patwardhan**

Portrait & Lifestyle Photography by
**Sangeet Ahuja**

# The World's Most Wanted Desserts

**With Vegan, Gluten Free and Dairy Free Options**

**By : Chef Harneet Jolly**

# Dedication _____

This book is dedicated to my grandfather
**Late Mr. Davinder Singh**

" Grandfather, smiling,
with his blue turban,
He continues to be our
inspiration,

His words of wisdom
and encouragement,
Enable us to face any
strenuous situation.

He is with us in spirit,
now and forever,
Giving us strength to
through difficulties
persevere.

His kindness, grace,
eloquence and humanity
continue to inspire us;
he was our friend and
our teacher."

# Chef Harpal Singh Sokhi _____

" Hello everyone this is your favourite Chef Harpal Singh Sokhi- the Energy Chef, Dancing Chef, Turban Tadka Chef, Jolly Good Chef and many more such titles that I have got from people, I thank all of them.

It gives me immense pleasure in writing this foreword for Chef Harneet Singh Jolly. Although I have not met him personally, his interests in baking are clearly visible in the content that he has written and shared in the book. The most important thing for any Chef is to have a book of his own which is a life time achievement and at such a young age Harneet has gone ahead and written a book which has some great recipes and his achievements.

I know for a fact that Baking, Patisserie and Mithai are a subject where you cannot manipulate, your recipes need to be absolutely perfect and the measurements cannot go wrong. You have to try and test them at least five times before you publish them and want people to try out the recipes. Harneet being a professional Chef has done all the hard work so that you don't fail in your kitchen any time you try and test the recipes of this beautiful book.

One of the most interesting parts of the book is where Harneet has shared various Icing that can be made professionally and at home. It is a sheer pleasure to do icing at home I feel that it is a perfect showcase of love while you are icing a cake. Apart from that you make various kinds of cookies, and one recipe that draws my attention is Jaggery and Fruit cake, a rare combination.

The book is a complete set of recipes drawn from the best of both the worlds, Indian and Western. Harneet has gone forward and added Indian drinks, a complete section of sauces for desserts which is rare, making it a must have book for all people who are aspiring to become Chefs.

I wish Harneet all the best and many more such books to come in future."

# Testimonials _

" Chef Harneet is a treasure to the culinary world. His in-depth knowledge and passion are a winning combination and an inspiration for the next generation of chefs."

———

## Chef Vikas Khanna

**Celebrity chef, Cookbook writer, Filmmaker, MasterChef judge**

" I am so proud to see Harneet's work and he is a true example of relentless hard work and passion. His book just doesn't talk about the classics but has his innovative twists in the recipes which makes it a must buy. His lineage is a proof of the pudding that his very thorough training will go with him a very long way. I wish him much success in each of his endeavour. God bless him."

## Chef Ajay Chopra

**Celebrity chef, Master Chef India S1 & S2 Judge**

" As baking and sweets require the technical precision of a good recipe, often times baking books and the recipes within feel like a boring instruction manual for a piece of shoddy furniture. What Chef Harneet has done is create a book that drips with passion and enthusiasm for the world of reward dessert! When I saw the chai biscuits shaped like tea bags, I knew this would be a book unlike any other."

## Chef Justin Warner

**Food Network Star winner and author of The Laws of Cooking: And How to Break Them**

" Butter, sugar, flour, and …. Magic, find the secrets in this sweet book."

___

## Chef Logan Guleff

**Masterchef Junior, America- Winner and cookbook author**

" Harneet Jolly proves to have great talent and skilful creativity. The use of fresh seasonal ingredients has always been delightful to all of my senses…the eyes that see the beautiful creation, the nose that takes in all the aroma ingredients emit, the ears to hear friends and family enjoying a meal or a dessert or a cocktail, the touch of hospitality that creates memories and of course the mouth that delights in all of the fine work of chefs around the world. Enjoy!"

## Chef Nancy Fuller

**Celebrity Chef, Food Network and author**

" As a man who is known to often order another steak for dessert, rather than something sweet, it is a tribute to Chef Harneet Jolly's skills as a pastry chef that I found this book so hugely enjoyable. I was particularly pleased to see a selection of some of my favourite Indian treats, which reminded me of the tastes of my Anglo Indian childhood. This is definitely a book that any would be dessert chef should add to their library"

## Chef Simon Majumdar

**Celebrity author, food writer, Iron Chef Judge**

# Meet Niranjan Patwardhan

*Photographer and Food Stylist*

Niranjan Patwardhan's passion for photography was ignited in his home-town of Pune, where he developed a profound fascination for the Western Ghats' wildlife and forests. He embarked on his photographic journey capturing these natural wonders with a keen eye for detail and a penchant for storytelling.

With a Bachelor's degree in Geology from Fergusson College, Pune, and a Master's degree in Geo-informatics from Pune University, Niranjan brings a unique perspective to his craft. Since 2019, he has been an integral part of the advertising photography industry, specializing primarily in fashion and beauty genres while nurturing a interest in food photography.

His portfolio boasts collaborations with some of the industry's biggest names.

Niranjan's photographic prowess has garnered international recognition, notably from prestigious fashion magazines such as Vogue Italia. He strives to seamlessly blend artistic creativity with technical expertise to capture the very essence of life itself growing through his lens.

# Meet Abha Baxi

*Graphic Designer and Illustrator*

Abha's creative journey began with an unwavering passion for art that was fueled from a young age. It was evident early on that art and design were not mere interests but her true calling.

Her innate artistic nature set her on a path that ultimately lead her to pursue a Fine Arts (Visual Communication) degree at Pune University. It was there that she honed her skills and nurtured her deep love for all things creative.

Her creative process is a blend of tradition and modernity, where she seamlessly applies and experiments with traditional art, infusing it with a contemporary and innovative approach.

For Abha, creation is not solely about the final product; it's a profound and joyous journey in itself. Being a graphic designer her mantra is to empathize, ideate, experiment and implement. She believes that it is not just about aesthetics but functionality too.

This holistic approach to design is a reflection of her commitment to creating art and illustrations that serve a purpose.

> "A recipe is lifeless, the cook infuses it with soul

# Contents

# Introduction

Desserts are that oasis in the desert for a distressed soul – be it a cake, or ice cream, or a dish loaded with fresh seasonal fruits. Desserts transcend boundaries of country and region while simultaneously staying within them. Scrumptious and satisfying; yet for many desserts are the Everest of culinary world. With a collection of desserts – ranging from easy to complex, classic to innovative, each with a plethora of complex flavors to tantalize your senses this book is a must add to your kitchen library. You will find recipes that suit your dietary needs, satisfy your taste buds, awe your guests, and inspire you to explore desserts.
You, the reader, are encouraged to experiment and innovate, and make the recipes your own!

I am Chef Harneet Jolly, and I present to you my recipes for some of my favourite desserts. My journey in the culinary world started at quite a young age, in my mother's kitchen. Even now, the family recipe for fruit cake remains my favourite dessert, made with love and glazed with a healthy helping of nostalgia. Over the course of my culinary adventures, I have studied at Culinary Academy of India (Hyderabad) and George Brown College (Toronto, Canada). I have also been the recipient of the MEGA Achievers Award for advocacy for Food For All, and Best Rising Chef Award in the category of desserts and pastries, both in 2021. And I have also been a part of the world record holding team for the largest variety of breads displayed, and hold a record in OMG book of records for my gravity defying cakes, chocolate sculptures, and photo frame desserts. I have designed menus and made center pieces for award functions in Bollywood. This book is the fruit of my training and efforts.

In a diverse nation like India with our unique culinary traditions and variety of cultures, I was introduced to the concept of dietary restrictions early on. My Sikh heritage teaches me the concept of Seva or selfless service. Building on those, and considering that in this globalized world, many of us for reasons of health, ethics, or beliefs, follow a variety of dietary restrictions, I have written this book. Indeed, it has been the core principle behind writing this book. I have taken into consideration such restrictions and created recipes suitable to vegetarian, vegan, gluten free, and dairy free diets.
Each recipe has been designed with utmost care and expert consultation so as to make them fit within the ambits of vegetarian, vegan, gluten free, and dairy free; and all recipes are marked according to the diet they fit into.

Options for modification are available to make them fit within your specific requirement. You may be a novice, or you may be a professional chef – with its precise measurements, tips, tricks, and options to modify, you will be able to create impressive desserts whenever you want! It doesn't matter if you're vegetarian or vegan, or if you can't eat dairy or gluten – there is a fantastic dessert in this book just for you!

# Who Am I?

Cooking has always been a pleasure for me, baking even more so. I was in the fourth grade, when I baked my first cake; of course, with the help of my mother; from whom I learnt to bake. From my great grandmother to my grandmother to my mother, this has come to me. Can you imagine the pride I feel to think that I could become the part of this family tradition, a heritage almost, to carry forward the traditional recipe of cake that has passed over from one generation to another? Even though I know now that the appreciation I got at that time for baking the cake was more to encourage me than the fact that the cake itself was really good, it was a pivotal moment in my life after which I never looked back and cooking became my passion.

I began to bake more cakes and improved over time. I can remember the time when I got genuine appreciation for the cake that I also felt was really good. However, that was just one step along the arduous path upon which I had to tread. Now, I practiced making some designer cakes and try my hand at a few other things. My desire to make cakes in new shapes and designs accidentally brought me to the Ultimate Cake Show on the TLC channel. Watching the masters making cakes on TV made me realise that it was not just baking a cake; rather it was an art; and that brought a remarkable change within me. It gave me the idea to use skeletal models and make gravity defying cakes.

I began to fuse two or more recipes of different dishes, studied their concepts and flavors, and began to create my own dish. My passion for cooking had now reached its peak and I seriously began to consider making it my career. The simple course of Hotel Management, however did not appeal to me and I began to search for some kind of special course in baking. My search took me to various places but finally reached its destination at CAI, (Culinary Art of India), Hyderabad whose alumni I am, and currently am a student of Advanced French Patisserie at the George Brown College, Toronto.

There is no denying the fact that the college proved to be outstanding and played a vital role in embellishing my skills. Taking part in the competition of 'Largest Varieties of Breads Displayed', which successfully managed to get itself recorded in Guinness Books of World Records with 493 varieties of breads, added another feather to my hat.

# Advice for ambitious cooks _____

Before You Get Started, let's have a look at some tips and tricks that will help you make your cooking experience really easy. Cooking and baking can be a real fun. The praises and appreciations that we get from others is an immense satisfaction, but that's not all there to this beautiful art. It is also very technical and relies heavily on precision, whether ingredients or steps. Sometimes, despite our best efforts, the desserts we make may not look like the one we wanted, and I'm here to help you avoid this disappointment. Apart from following the recipe correctly, these are some tips and tricks that need to be observed as well.

**1. Read the recipe carefully** – Before you try your hand at a recipe, read it word by word a few times. Try and visualize each step in your mind and be sure you know each ingredient. This way, the chances of errors will be reduced.

**2. Organise the ingredients properly** – assemble all the ingredients needed for the recipe before you begin to cook. If possible, measure out ingredients beforehand and keep them ready. The recipe will then be very simple to follow with everything to hand.

**3. Use ingredients at correct temp** – please ensure all the ingredients are at room temperature, especially eggs and butter, unless stated otherwise. For creaming, the butter needs to be soft and will not work if you are using cold butter. If cold, it will not emulsify as needed and would also not trap enough air. However, the cream would immediately split upon whipping if it's not cold. The butter for crumbles and pies should be cold and solid, as stated in the recipes.

**4. Measure your ingredients right** – measure all the ingredients with care because few minutes spent on proper measurements will be an insurance against wasted efforts. Do not cut or increase recipe quantities unless you have acquired enough experience.

Standard spoon measurements are used in all recipes.

1 tablespoon (tbsp) =15ml spoon

1 teaspoon (tsp) = 5ml spoon

All spoons' measurements are leveled.

**5. Best quality ingredients** – The better the ingredients, the better will be the dish. The quality of ingredients makes a huge difference to how your desserts turn out. I use regular salted Amul Butter for all my dishes, unless otherwise stated. The whipping cream I prefer is non-dairy due to its longer shelf life and stability. I usually use all purpose flour for all the recipes as it gives the fluffiest and lightest results. To make almond meal or almond flour, process whole almonds in the food processor and sieve it once. Make sure to not process them too long otherwise it will release its oil. Use freshly ground spices where ever mentioned.

**6. Right material for baking** – you will be surprised to see how much difference the bake wares make. I usually prefer metal bake ware as metal is a good conductor of heat. However, Glass being a poor conductor of heat; cakes should not be baked in it. If a dessert needs to be served in the dish or eaten out of the dish, glass or ceramic is ideal.

**7. Keep oven doors closed** – you may be tempted often to open the oven and have a look at the dish, but doing this is not a good idea. Opening the door rapidly drops the temperature and can result in a deflated cake. Hence keep the door closed and open only to rotate the tray or check if the dessert is done.

**8. Rest, chill and do not hurry** – a lot of recipes require the dough to be chilled, which is an essential step and should never be skipped. While preparing pies and cookies, chilling the dough makes it firm enough to be handled and rolled to a sheet easily. After lining the pie dish with the dough, chilling it again reduces the shrinkage.

**9. Be patient** – preparing desserts require a lot of patience. Make sure you have enough time at hand before starting the recipe. Once the cake or brownie or any other dessert has baked, be patient and let them cool completely in the moulds/ trays. Hot products are more likely to break apart. Also make sure to frost the cakes only once they are properly cooled down. Resting them in freezer for an hour is even better if possible.

# Kitchen Gear

RECIPE:

Chocolate Cake

# Pantry essentials _____

The list of ingredients you can keep can be extremely huge and daunting, limited only by the space available. But you will be glad to know, the list can be narrowed down to some essential, must have ingredients which should always be present in your pantry. While writing this book, I've tried to use ingredients which are readily available. A small advice before you start reading the list is to use only the best quality of ingredients. Yes, that makes a huge difference!

**Flours:**

1. All purpose flour – a super versatile flour which can be used to make almost anything from cookies to cakes to doughnuts.

2. Cornflour/ Cornstarch – A finely ground flour used for thickening sauces and pie fillings.

**How to store flour?**

Store flour in airtight, moisture proof container in cool and dark place, preferably in a refrigerator. Whole wheat flour spoils faster than all-purpose flour due to the presence of more components i.e. bran and germ.

**Note:** For best results, use the kind of flour specified in the recipe until you know how it will impact the outcome.

**Leaveners:**

Leaving is the air that causes bread, cakes and other products to rise when they are baked or fried. Each leavener has different purpose and outcome.
They can be divided into chemical and biological.

**Chemical Leaveners**

**1. Baking soda / sodium bi carbonate** – a chemical leavener which comes in small box, works only when it combines with an acid and produces a chemical reaction. Therefore, it should be used in dishes only if they contain any acidic ingredient such as lemon, yogurt, lemon juice etc.

**2. Baking powder** – It is a powder which contains sodium bi carbonate, an acidic agent (cream of tartar) and starch. Unlike sodium bi carbonate, it can be directly added to dish even if it does not contain any acidic ingredients.

**Biological leaveners**

**3. Yeast** – A biological leavener responsible for fermentation, hence, mainly used for doughs like breads and doughnuts. It takes longer than the chemical leaveners to act. I use instant dry active yeast which is a granular yeast sold in packets. Note: Be mindful that the leavening agents cannot be interchanged due to their properties, as the recipe would not work.

**Sweeteners:**

**1. Granulated sugar**- as the name suggests, this sugar comes in bigger granule and works perfectly fine for most of the recipes. It is obtained from sugarcane or beet and is processed to remove molasses, a by-product of sugar manufacturing often used for its color and flavor.

**2. Castor/ Fine/ breakfast sugar** – this sugar has much smaller granular size compared to the granulated sugar. Its tiny size helps to dissolve it quicker. This can be substituted 1:1 for granulated sugar.

**3. Icing sugar** – sugar ground into a very fine powder and is mixed with starch. It is used in frostings and icings. A quick dusting of this sugar can make any dessert look prettier.

**4. Brown sugar** – It is refined sugar with molasses added. It adds an extra to the dessert. To measure, press it tightly in the measuring cup or use a digital scale.

**5. Honey** – a sweet and sticky nectar brought to us by bees adds a unique flavor to your treats.

**Dairy and poultry:**

**1. Whipping cream** - When the recipe calls for whipping cream, I've used non dairy Rich's Gold whipping cream which already has sugar added. If replacing with a dairy cream, you might want to sweeten it with icing sugar.

**Note:** Using a cold bowl will give you better results while whipping.

**2. Cooking cream** - Recipes which require cooking cream, I use fresh cream by Amul available in tetra packs.

**3. Eggs** - Eggs are a must! Use regular eggs brought from local shop or the ones sold in boxes- both are good choices. Always use eggs at room temperature.

**Fats:**

**1. Vegetable oil** - Having a very neutral flavor, it doesn't overpower the product and creates a super moist texture.

**2. Butter** -I prefer using salted butter by Amul due to its flavor and availability. All the recipes in this book are created keeping the salt content of butter in mind. Whenever using unsalted butter, add a pinch of salt to the recipes.

**Chocolate:**

**1. Chocolate bar** – A must have ingredient! They can be used to make ganache, chocolate sauce, garnishes, dipping doughnuts and much more. My favourite brands are cacao barry and Lindt. However, they can be difficult to obtain. You can definitely go ahead with easily available Morde cooking chocolate.

**2. Cocoa powder** - Unsweetened cocoa powder is an essential whenever you want to create something chocolaty. I prefer using Dutch processed powder as it is darker in color and has a more mellow flavor.

**3. Choco chip** – Small tit bits when added to any dessert, makes it look extremely pretty. Keeping dark and white choco chips is advisable.

**Note:** Out of choco chips and can't run to the market? Chop chocolate bar into small pieces and use.

**Other:**

**1. Food colors** - They can be available in many different forms namely liquid, gel, powders, liqu gel etc but usually gel colors should be sufficient for most of your work. If you don't know how much color to add, start by adding only a little at a time. Mix it well and check. Add more if required.

**2. Sugar sprinkles** – Sugar sprinkles and decorating sugars can be used for topping any dessert whether it is ice cream or cake or mousse.

———————

# Biscuits & Cookies

| Recipes | Vegan | Gluten free | Dairy free |
|---|---|---|---|
| 1. Biscotti | | | ✓ |
| 2. Choco chip skillet cookies | ✓ | | ✓ |
| 3. Masala chai teabag biscuits | ✓ | | ✓ |
| 4. Nan khatai | | | |
| 5. Red velvet cookies | | | |
| 6. Soft centered nutella cookies | ✓ | | ✓ |

# Faults, reasons and remedies

| Faults | Possible reason | Remedy |
|---|---|---|
| Dough too sticky | Dough not thoroughly chilled | Let the dough chill in refrigerator for some more time. |
| Cookies too tough | Dough over mixed | Do not over handle the dough. Just mix it enough to combine. |
| Uneven baking | Hot and cold spots in oven | Rotate your tray halfway during the baking processing. |
| Cookies too oily | Butter too soft | Use cold butter unless stated in the recipe. |
| Cookies spreading too much | Baking tray too warm | Place cookies on a cool baking tray. |
| Cookies not spreading enough | Dough too tough | Do not knead the dough. Just mix enough to combine it together. <br><br> Adding 1-2tbsp milk should help. |
| Cookies pale on top but burnt on bottom | Oven too hot | Try reducing the temperature by 10°C to see if you get better results. |
| Cookies are too thin and crisp (in case of red velvet cookies) | Dough not chilled enough | Chilling the dough after diving should fix this problem. |
| Biscotti are hard instead of crisp | Dough not chilled enough | Chilling the dough after diving should fix this problem. |

# Biscotti

" The word biscotti, in Italian, means twice baked and double baking is the secret to its dry and crunchy texture which makes it perfect for dunking into your hot coffee or tea."

Prep: 80 min

Cook: 30 min

Serves: 6

Total: 120 min

# Ingredients

200g All-purpose flour

1tbsp Milk powder

1/2tsp Baking powder

A pinch Baking soda

130g Castor sugar

70g Butter

A pinch Salt

1/4tsp Vanilla extract

1no. Eggs

20g Pistachio nuts (chopped)

20g Walnuts (chopped)

20g Candid cherry(chopped)

———

# Method

1. Line a baking tray with butter paper and keep aside.

2. Sift together flour, milk powder, baking powder and baking soda.

3. Beat together sugar, butter, salt and vanilla extract until smooth, about 2-3 minutes. Add egg and beat for another minute.

4. Stir in the flour mixture and chopped nuts until combined and forms dough. Tightly wrap the dough in a cling wrap and refrigerate till hard, about 20 minutes.

5. Form the dough into a log. Place on the baking sheet and freeze for 30 minutes.

6. Bake in a preheated oven at 160°C/ 325°F for 35 minutes or until golden brown.  Allow to cool for about 10 minutes.

7. Put the logs on a chopping board and slice into 1/4th inch thickness. Arrange them back on the baking tray and bake for another 5-6 minutes on each side.

8. Transfer to a wire rack to cool down.

## Made extra and don't know what to do?

Made extra and don't know what to do? This freezes up very well. You can make this recipe ahead and store in freezer so that you always have these delicious cookies on hand. All you have to do is to let the logs cool completely after step 6 and wrap into cling wrap nicely. Freeze for up to a month. Proceed with step 7 whenever you need the biscotti.

For a Dairy free option, you can skip adding the milk powder as it is only for flavor purpose.

# Choco Chip Skillet Cookie

" A warm, gooey giant sized cookie served with ice-cream is all you need when your friends have come over. Skip the plates, grab the spoons, dig into this cookie and make any moment a memory."

Prep: 40 min    Cook: 10 min    Serves: 4    Total: 50 min

## Ingredients

100g All-purpose flour

1tbsp Dutch processed cocoa powder

1/4tsp Baking soda

100g Castor sugar

85g Butter

A pinch Salt

1/4tsp Vanilla extract

2tbsp Milk

15g Choco chips

## To Serve

Tastes best with vanilla ice cream

Chocolate fudge sauce (refer recipe on pg 157) Honey

## To Serve

1. Sift together flour, cocoa powder and baking soda.

2. Beat together sugar, butter, salt and vanilla extract until smooth, about 2-3 minutes. Add milk and beat for another minute. Stir in the flour mixture and Choco chips until combined and forms dough.

3. Tightly wrap the dough in a cling wrap and refrigerate till hard, about 20 minutes.

4. Divide the dough into 4 equal parts and flatten the dough in 8 inch skillets.

5. Bake in a preheated oven at 180°C/ 350°F for 12 minutes.

6. Serve warm with Refrigerator vanilla ice cream drizzled with chocolate fudge sauce and honey.

### Note

To make this recipe vegan, replace the butter with margarine and regular milk with soy milk.

Keep the quantities same.

If you ran out of choco-chips, use chocolate chunks chopped to the size of choco-chips.

# Masala Chai Teabag Biscuits

" The word biscotti, in Italian, means twice baked and double baking is the secret to its dry and crunchy texture which makes it perfect for dunking into your hot coffee or tea."

Prep: 75 min.

Cook: 12 min.

Serves: 8

Total: 90 min.

———

## Ingredients

60ml Water

4tbsp Tea leaves

60g Butter (chilled, cubed)

100g All-purpose flour

30g Castor sugar

1/8tsp Baking powder

Ground spices

1/4tsp Cardamom

1/4tsp Cardamom

1/4tsp Cinnamon

1/4tsp Dry ginger

1/4tsp Black pepper

**To Garnish:** white chocolate (melted), String and label

___

## Method

1. In a saucepan, boil water and tea leaves until it is reduced to 1/4th. Remove from heat, strain and keep it aside.

2. Place the chilled butter, flour, castor sugar, baking powder and spices in a food processor and pulse until it resembles bread crumbs. Then add the tea decoction, one spoon at a time and pulse until it starts to gather. Do not knead the dough.

3. Wrap the dough with cling film and rest for 15-20 minutes in refrigerator.

4. On a lightly floured surface, roll the dough to a thickness of about 2mm. Cut the dough into teabag shape using a cookie cutter or a sharp knife and transfer to a baking sheet. Using a round nozzle, poke a hole at the top of each cookie and put the tray in the refrigerator for 30 minutes.

5. Bake the cookies in a preheated oven at 200°C/ 400°F for 12 minutes or till slightly golden. Allow to cool down completely.

6. Dip the tea bag cookies halfway in the melted chocolate and let the chocolate set. Use string and label to decorate.

### Note

Make this recipe vegan by replacing butter with equal amount of margarine.

It may take one or two tries to get the shape right, but even if they don't look perfect, they will still taste delicious. Once they are cool enough to eat, you will understand that looks aren't everything.

# Nan Khatai

"A warm, gooey giant sized cookie served with ice-cream is all you need when your friends have come over. Skip the plates, grab the spoons, dig into this cookie and make any moment a memory."

Prep: 15 min

Cook: 12 min

Serves: 6

Total: 30 min

## Ingredients

100g All-purpose flour

25g Chickpea flour

1/4tsp Ground cardamom

60g Ghee (clarified butter)

50g Powdered sugar

A few strands Saffron

25g Pistachios (chopped)

———

## Method

1. Sieve together flour, chickpea flour and ground cardamom. Keep aside.

2. Cream ghee, sugar and saffron together till light and fluffy, about 5 minutes. Then add the flour mixture and mix using your hand until it gathers together.

3. Divide the dough into 15 gram balls and flatten them a little using your hand. Press some chopped pistachios in the center and place them on a greased baking tray.

4. Bake in a preheated oven at 200°C / 400°F for 10-12 minutes.

5. Serve at room temperature.

### Note

Use unsalted butter if ghee is not available; however it will change the taste completely.

# Red Velvet Cookies

"These are perfectly soft and chewy, gorgeously red and dotted with white chocolate chips. These would go great on Christmas or Valentine Day."

Prep: 95 min

Cook: 15 min

Serves: 6

Total: 110 min

## Ingredients

150g All-purpose flour

1tbsp Corn starch

1tsp Dutch processed cocoapowder

1/4tsp Baking powder

A pinch Baking soda

80g Castor sugar

60g Butter

A pinch Salt

1/8tsp Vanilla extract

1tbsp Curd

1tsp Synthetic vinegar

1tsp Red food color

30g White Choco chips

---

## Method

1. Line a baking tray with butter paper and keep aside.

2. Sift together flour, corn starch, cocoa powder, baking powder and baking soda.

3. Beat together sugar, butter, salt and vanilla extract until smooth, about 2-3 minutes. Add curd, vinegar and red food color. Beat for another minute. Stir in the flour mixture and Choco chips until combined and forms dough.

4. Tightly wrap the dough in a cling wrap and refrigerate till hard, about 30 minutes. Divide the dough into 20 gram balls. Place on the prepared baking tray.

5. Bake in a preheated oven at 180°C/ 350°F for 10 minutes.

6. Let it cool for 10 minutes and transfer to a wire rack until completely cooled.

## Note

**Why not try a different color and make it blue velvet or yellow velvet cookie and so on?**

Add the food color of your choice, a little at a time, stirring to incorporate each addition until you have the desired result. You can skip adding color for white velvet cookie.

# Soft Centered Nutella Cookies

"An unassuming chocolate cookie that hides a chocolaty secret.
Take a bite and you will drown in delicious nutella"

Prep: 95 min

Cook: 10min

Serves: 6

Total: 110 min

———

# Ingredients

**Filling:**

160g Nutella

**Cookie dough:**

200g All-purpose flour

1tbsp Corn starch

2tbsp Dutch processed cocoa powder

2.5 tsp Instant coffee powder

1/4tsp Baking soda

200g Castor sugar

170g Butter

A pinch Salt

1/4tsp Vanilla extract

4tbsp Milk

——

# Method

1. Line a small tray with butter paper and pipe 10 gram dollops of nutella. Put the tray in deep freezer for 30 minutes.

2. Line 2 baking trays with butter paper and keep aside.

3. Sift together flour, corn starch, cocoa powder, coffee powder and baking soda.

4. Beat together sugar, butter, salt and vanilla extract until smooth, about 2-3 minutes. Add milk and beat for another minute. Stir in the flour mixture until combined and forms dough.

5. Tightly wrap the dough in a cling wrap and refrigerate till hard, about 30 minutes.

6. Take 35 gram dough, gently flatten it and place a nutella ball on top, then wrap the dough to seal it completely. Roll into a ball and put on the baking tray. Repeat with rest of the material keeping the cookie balls at least 1 inch apart from each other.

7. Bake in a preheated oven at 180°C/ 350°F for 10 minutes. Let it cool / completely before removing it from the tray.

### Note

Replace butter with equal amount of margarine to make these cookies vegan or dairy free. Regular milk can be replaced by either soy or almond milk. There are various vegan alternatives to nutella, which can be used for this recipe.

These cookies may seem exceptionally soft after 10 minutes of baking, but they will set once cooled.

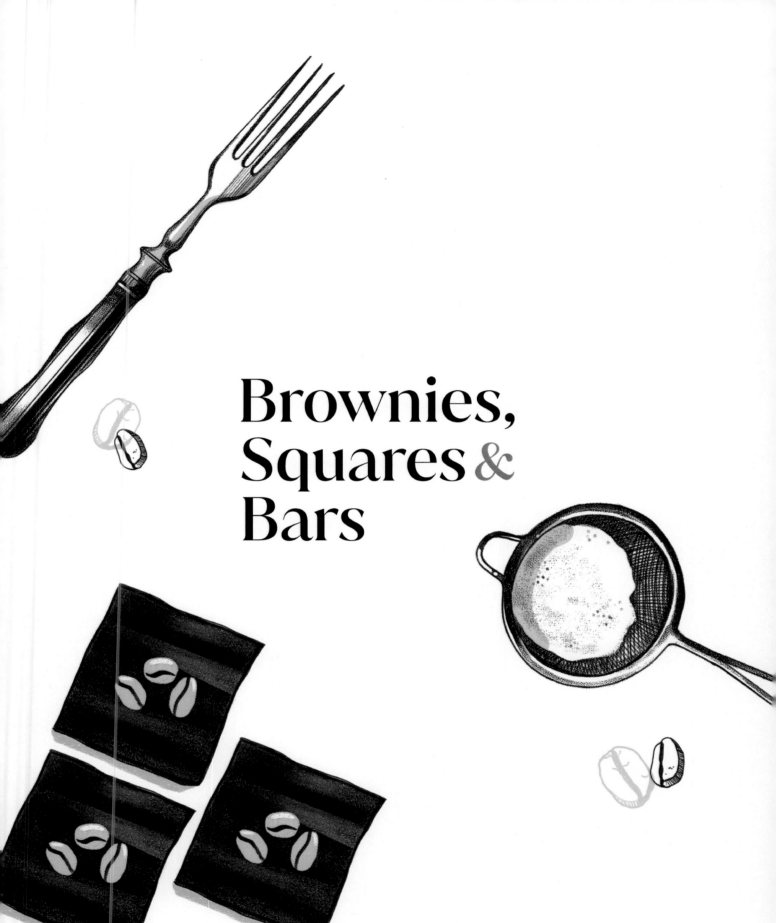

# Brownies,
# Squares &
# Bars

| Recipes | Vegan | Gluten free | Dairy free |
|---|---|---|---|
| 1. Lemon tart bars | | | ✓ |
| 2. Chocolate caramel fudge bite | | ✓ | |
| 3. Homemade muesli and nuts bar | ✓ | ✓ | ✓ |
| 4. Orange crumble | ✓ | | ✓ |
| 5. Walnut brownie | | | ✓ |

# Lemon Tart Bars

" These not so traditional lemon tart bars have a crumbly, cookie like crust and set lemon curd. These have been favourite in my family for years."

Prep: 80 min

Cook: 10 min

Serves: 8

Total: 90 min

———

## Ingredients

**Base:**

50g Butter

100g All-purpose flour

25g Powdered sugar

1tbsp Ice cold water

**Lemon Topping:**

1/2tbsp Gelatine

70ml Water

4no. Egg yolks

100g Castor sugar

60ml Lemon Juice

1tsp Lemon Zest

**To garnish:**

Mint sprig

---

## Method

**Base:**

1. Line a 9x5 inch rectangle cake pan with aluminium foil.

2. Follow the first 3 steps of pie crust recipe :

a) Cut the cold butter in chunks and place it on kitchen counter.

b) Sieve flour and sugar on top and cut the butter further using a dough scrapper until the mixture resembles breadcrumbs.

c) Add ice cold water a spoon at a time and mix until dough gathers itself into a ball. Wrap the dough tightly in a cling wrap and chill for an hour.

3. On a lightly floured surface, roll the dough to a thickness of about 1/8th inch. Press the dough in the prepared cake pan and prick using a fork.

4. Bake in a preheated oven at 200°C/ 390°F for 10 minutes or until golden brown.

**Bloom the gelatine:**

1. In a microwave safe bowl, add gelatine and water. Mix well using a spoon and let it rest for 10 minutes or until water is fully absorbed.

**Lemon Topping:**

1. Add egg yolks, sugar, lemon juice and lemon zest to a bowl.

2. Put over a double boiler and cook till thickened. Stir constantly or egg yolk may cook unevenly and get curdled.

3. Remove from the heat and add melted gelatine. Mix thoroughly and pass it through a mesh.

4. Pour this mixture over the base and let it set in refrigerator at least for an hour.

5. Cut in bars and serve garnished with mint sprig.

**Note:**

If you are not a fan of gelatine or want a vegetarian replacement, use the same amount of agar-agar powder in the recipe and add it with rest of the ingredients while making the lemon topping. It is very important to cook the agar-agar to activate its gelatinous properties. Butter can be replaced with margarine for a dairy free option.

# Chocolate Caramel Fudge Bites

"This is a perfect bite sized treat requiring very few ingredients and time. No candy thermometer is required to make these candies and it comes out perfect every time."

Prep: 15 min    Cook: 5 min    Serves: 6    Total: 20 min

## Ingredients

120g Condensed milk

90g Brown sugar

50g Butter

1tbsp Golden syrup

100g White chocolate (finely chopped)

100g Semisweet chocolate

___

## Method

1. Line a 5x9inch rectangle cake tin with aluminium foil. Keep aside.

2. In a heavy bottomed pan, add condensed milk, brown sugar, butter and golden syrup. Cook it on simmer till thickened, around 5 minutes.

3. Remove the pan from heat and add the chopped white chocolate.

Stir well until the chocolate melts completely.

4. Transfer the fudge mixture to the prepared cake pan and let it set hard in refrigerator.

5. Once set, pour melted semisweet chocolate over the fudge and let it set too.

6. Cut into small squares and serve.

### Are you looking for fudge storage idea?

After all, no one would want their creamy fudge to get crumbly or lose taste. Store it in an air-tight glass container in a dark and cool place for about a week. Heat from the sun will spoil it faster. Hence, the best suited place is a cupboard.

# Homemade Muesli and Nuts Bar

" The homemade muesli and nut bars are a smart and delicious way to start your day. These coconut-y bars are filled with flavors and packed with proteins. The nuts make a perfect dessert- like breakfast to go."

Prep: 30 min

Cook: 10 min

Serves: 8

Total: 40 min

# Ingredients

50g Instant oats

25g Cornflakes

1tbsp Sesame seeds

1tbsp Melon seeds

20g Almond flakes

1tbsp Flax seeds

50g Desiccated coconut

20g Raisins

20g Sultanas

20g Candid cherry

120g Butter

100g Honey

2tbsp Brown sugar

————

# Method

**Base:**

1. Line a 9x5 inch rectangle cake pan with butter paper. Set aside.

2. In a large pan over low heat, toast oats and cornflakes. Transfer to a mixing bowl.

3. Lightly roast sesame seeds, melon seeds, almond flakes and flax seeds till aromatic and golden brown. Transfer this to a mixing bowl as well.

4. Separately roast desiccated coconut and add it to rest of the ingredients in the mixing bowl.

5. Also add raisins, sultanas and candid cherry. Let the mixture cool down.

6. In a small saucepan over low heat, cook butter, honey and brown sugar till sugar dissolves, about 2-3 minutes.

7. Bring to a boil; reduce heat to low, without stirring, cook for another 4 minutes. Add this hot mixture to the dry ingredients and mix well.

8. Spoon the mixture into the prepared cake pan and press firmly with the back of a wooden spoon. Allow to cool down completely.

**To serve:**

1. Cut into bars and dust with confectioner's sugar.

### Note

To make this recipe vegan, replace butter with margarine and honey with maple syrup.

There are various options in the market for gluten free oats and cornflakes.

You can vary the nuts and seeds according to your taste and what you have on hand keeping the total quantities of nuts and seeds the same.

# Orange Crumble

"Orange crumbles are a perfect blend of textures. They have a crunchy crumble top and slightly chewy orange filling giving the bars a fresh zesty flavor."

Prep: 25 min     Cook: 40 min     Serves: 6     Total: 65 min

## Ingredients

100g All-purpose flour

50g Castor sugar

A pinch Salt

50g Butter

120g Orange marmalade

___

## Method

1. Preheat the oven to 180°C/ 350°F. Line a baking tray with parchment paper.

2. Process all-purpose flour, sugar and salt in a food processor for a few seconds. Add butter and pulse until mixture becomes crumbly and resembles coarse meal.

(A dough cutter could be used if food processor is not available.)

3. Press half of the crumble dough into the bottom of the prepared tray. Transfer to the oven and bake for 10 minutes or until slightly golden.

4. Take out the tray and spoon the orange marmalade over the pre-baked crust. Sprinkle the remaining crumble dough overtop the marmalade.

5. Return to the oven and bake for 30-40 minutes or until crumbles are golden brown.

6. Let it cool completely. Cut into squares and dust with confectioner's sugar.

### Note

Replace butter with margarine to make this recipe vegan and dairy free.

# Walnut Brownie

" These walnut brownies are ultra-rich, super fudgy, moist, chewy and loaded with walnuts. These are the perfect treat for almost every occasion."

Prep: 20 min

Cook: 40 min

Serves: 6

Total: 60 min

## Ingredients

125g All-purpose flour

A pinch Baking powder

20g Cocoa powder

30ml Water

160g Sugar

80g Butter

230g Semisweet chocolate

2no. Eggs

30g Walnuts (chopped, divided)

———

## Method

1. Line the cake tin with butter paper.

2. Sift together flour, baking powder and cocoa powder. Keep aside.

3. Boil water, sugar and butter in a small pan. Remove from heat and stir in chopped chocolate.

4. Once melted completely, add in the eggs and mix well. Now add the flour mixture and mix till smooth.

5. Add half the chopped walnuts into the batter and pour it into the prepared cake pan. Sprinkle remaining walnuts on top.

6. Bake in a preheated oven at 200°C/400°F for 40 minutes. Cool down completely before serving.

## Note

For a dairy free option, replace butter with margarine.

Why stop at walnuts if you can add so many more interesting things to it? It you are spending some quality baking time, why not try small chunks of coconut, butter cookies, choco-chips, peanut butter chips or even savoury bits of crispy bacon, salted peanuts, pumpkin seeds. Let your imagination be your guide.

Making brownie requires only the most basic equipment. If you are tempted to use a stand mixer, I would suggest sticking to a hand mixer as overbeating the eggs in this recipe can introduce too much air resulting in a cakey rather than a fudgy brownie.

# Cakes

| Recipes | Vegan | Gluten free | Dairy free |
|---|---|---|---|
| 1. Black velvet cake | | | |
| 2. Brown butter hazelnut cake | | | |
| 3. Dense bitter eggless cake | | | |
| 4. Honey raisin oatmeal cake | | | ✓ |
| 5. Lemon and fig cake | | | |

# Faults, reasons and remedies

| Faults | Possible reason | Remedy |
|---|---|---|
| Cake rose unevenly | Batter spread unevenly | Spread batter evenly |
| | Baking tray / pan not leveled | Adjust the tray level |
| Sunken cake | Oven not hot enough | Preheat oven to correct temperature |
| | Oven door opened before the cake sets. | Use cold butter unless stated in the recipe. |
| | Underbaked | Bake thoroughly |
| Cracked top | Oven temperature too hot | Check the oven temperature |
| | Too much rising agent | Follow the recipe correctly |
| Cake stuck to the pan | Baking tin not greased well | Grease the pan well or use parchment paper to line. |
| Top burned, middle not done yet | Oven temperature too hot | Chilling the dough after diving should fix this problem. |
| | Cake tin too small | Fill the pan maximum upto 3/4th of its height. |
| Very dense | Improper mixing | Mix the batter well. |
| | Not enough rising agent | Follow the recipe correctly |
| Cake too tough | Over mixing | Do not over mix the batter |
| | Batter too stiff | Add more liquid. Addition of a little milk can help. |
| Cake too tough | Baked too long | Keep a check on timing |
| Cake overflowing | Cake pan filled too much | A good rule of thumb is to fill a cake pan 2/3rd of its height. |

# Black Velvet Cake

"Black velvet cake is the perfect and royal twist to the common red velvet cake we love. It is a super moist cake with just a hint of cocoa flavor and tart cream cheese frosting."

 Prep: 90 min  Cook: 30 min  Serves: 8  Total: 120 min

## Ingredients

**Cake:**

175g All-purpose flour

1tsp Baking powder

1/2tsp Baking soda

1tbsp Dutch processed cocoa powder

3no. Eggs

175g Granulated sugar

1tsp Black food color (gel based)

125ml Buttermilk

175ml Oil

A pinch Salt

2tsp Synthetic vinegar

## Method

**Cake:**

1. Line two 6 inch cake pans with butter paper.

2. Sieve together flour, baking powder, baking soda and cocoa powder. Keep aside.

3. Beat eggs and sugar with a stand or hand mixer for about 5-6 minutes or till no sugar crystals are visible. Stir in the black food color, buttermilk, oil, salt and vinegar. Add flour mixture and mix at a very low speed.

4. Pour the batter in the prepared cake pan and bake in a preheated oven at 180°C/ 350°F for 30 minutes, till skewer inserted comes out clean.

5. Cool it completely in the pan before removing it.

## Ingredients

Frosting:

200g Cream cheese frosting
(refer recipe on pg 79)

1/2tsp Black gel food color

Filling:

200g Cream cheese frosting
(refer recipe on pg 79)

## Method

Frosting:

1. Take chocolate cream cheese
frosting and mix in black food color.

To assemble:

1. Cut each cake horizontally into
two layers. To fill, put a dollop of
cream cheese frosting and spread
evenly. Place another layer of cake
and repeat till all the four layers
are used. Frost the whole cake with
black cream cheese.

Choc Cream
Cheese

Cream Cheese

Black Velvet Cake

### Note

Piping nozzles come in variety
of shapes and sizes. You can
get really creative with these
nozzles to decorate a cake. It
may take some practice to get
the designs right but they are
worth the extra effort. You can
always practice on an inverted
cake pan before starting on the
cake; and remember, if you are
unhappy, you can always scrape
it off and start all over again.

While icing, try not to let your
scraper come in contact with
the cake as it will pick up the
crumbs making the frosting
look messy.

# Brown Butter Hazelnut Cake

"In this simple yet elegant Brown butter hazelnut cake, the browned butter adds a unique nutty flavor complementing the flavor of hazelnuts beautifully."

Prep: 25 min          Cook: 40 min          Serves: 6          Total: 65 min

# Brown Butter Hazelnut Cake

## Ingredients

150g Butter

150g All-purpose flour

1tsp Baking powder

3no. Eggs

150g Brown sugar

1/4tsp vanilla extract

50g Hazelnuts (powdered)

50g Hazelnuts (cut into halves)

**To serve:**

Sweetened cream

———

## Method

1. Line a tea cake loaf pan with butter paper.

2. Add butter to a pan and heat it over medium heat until brown, about 5 min. Let it cool.

3. Sift flour and baking powder in another bowl. Keep side.

4. In a mixer blender, put eggs, brown sugar, browned butter and vanilla extract. Blend till the sugar dissolves and the mixture becomes completely smooth.

5. Add the flour mixture and hazelnut powder. Pulse it for 2– 3 times until combined. Add half cut hazelnuts and combine lightly. Transfer it to the cake pan and flatten the top.

6. Bake in a preheated oven at 180°C/ 350°F for 40-45 minutes. Let it cool completely. Dip the top in melted chocolate and cover with hazelnuts.

7. Slice and serve with sweetened cream.

## Note

The brown butter used in this cake recipe really takes the taste to another level.

However, you can use regular butter if you don't want to do the added step.

# Dense Bitter Eggless Cake

> " This chocolate cake is the only recipe you would ever need. It's moist, rich, delicious and moreover eggless. I've been making this recipe from the time I started baking, with a few twists here and there. It has never let me down, whether it's served along with tea or carved and draped with fondant for a novelty cake."

Prep: 15 min

Cook: 45 min

Serves: 8

Total: 120 min

# Dense Bitter Eggless Cake

## Ingredients

200g All-purpose flour

50g Dutch processed cocoa powder

3tsp Baking powder

1/2tsp Baking soda

100g Butter

400g Condensed milk

60g Castor sugar

1/4tsp Vanilla extract

120g 80% dark chocolate

**Frosting:**

50ml Sugar syrup

300g Chocolate ganache

———

## Method

1. Line two 7inch cake pans with butter paper.

2. Sift flour, cocoa powder, baking powder and baking soda. Keep aside.

3. Beat together butter, condensed milk, sugar and vanilla extract till all the sugar dissolves. Stir in the melted chocolate.

4. Add the flour and mix using a whisk until no lumps are left. Transfer the batter to the prepared pans.

5. Bake in a preheated oven at 180°C/350°F for 40- 45 minutes until the skewer inserted comes out clean.

6. Cool for 15 minutes before removing from the pan. Cool completely over the wire rack.

**To assemble:**

1. Cut each cake horizontally into two layers and lightly moisten with sugar syrup using a pastry brush.

2. Put a dollop of chocolate ganache frosting and spread evenly. Top with another layer of cake and moisten with syrup. Repeat till all the layers are used.

3. Now crumb coat the cake and refrigerate for 10 minutes. Then frost and decorate using the ganache as desired.

# Dense Bitter
# Eggless Cake

Chocolate Ganache

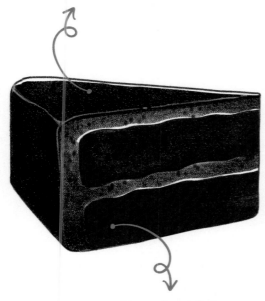

Chocolate Cake

## Note

Crumb coating is a thin layer of frosting applied to a cake to seal all the crumbs in. It is a stepworth extra time. It will ensure that no crumbs show up in the final frosting when you ice the cake giving it a super smooth finish.

To apply a crumb coat, simply use a pallete knife or an offset spatula to spread a thin layer of the frosting over the sides and top of the cake.

Refrigerate for about 10 minutes or until the crumb coat is set before you apply the final frosting.

# Jaggery, Fruit and Tamarind Cake

> " A moist and super delicious jaggery and fruit cake with a tang of tamarind packed with dried fruits. This colorful cake is a wonderful choice to lighten up any festival or holiday."

Prep: 10 min

Cook: 45 min

Serves: 6

Total: 60 min

# Ingredients

150g All-purpose flour

1.5tsp Baking powder

1/2tsp Baking soda

150g Butter (salted)

180g Jaggery (grated)

1/4tsp vanilla extract

1tsp Tamarind pulp

3no. Eggs

20g Almonds (chopped)

20g Cashew nuts (chopped)

20g Walnuts (chopped)

20g Apricot (dried)

20g Candied cherries

20g Candid papaya

20g Raisins

20g Sultanas

---

# Method

1. Line a tea cake pan with butter paper.

2. Sift flour, baking powder and baking soda. Keep aside.

3. Beat together butter and grated jaggery using a stand or a hand mixer until light and fluffy. Add vanilla extract, tamarind pulp and eggs, one at a time. Whisk till combined completely.

4. Add flour mixture, keeping aside 1tsp. for later use. Mix till a smooth batter is formed.

5. Put chopped nuts and fruits in a bowl and coat them with the reserved flour. Put it in the batter and fold. Transfer the batter to the prepared cake pan.

6. Bake in a preheated oven at 180°C/ 350°F for 45 minutes, until it passes the skewer test.

7. Cool down completely before serving.

## Note

When adding dried fruits, make sure to cut the larger fruits like apricots to match the size of small fruits like raisins and sultanas for equal distribution. However, you shouldn't be scared to use whole fruits on the top for aesthetic reasons.

Jaggery adds an amazing flavor and color to this recipe. However, if you don't have it, you can use 150g of regular brown sugar or even granulated sugar in place of 180g jaggery.

# Lemon and Fig Cake

"So easy to make and so delicious to eat! This moist, tender and brightly flavored lemon cake is perfectly paired with the earthy sweet figs.

 Prep: 15min

 Cook: 45 min

 Serves: 6

 Total: 60 min

## Ingredients

100g All-purpose flour

1tsp Baking powder

1/4tsp Baking soda

3no. Eggs

80g Granulated Sugar

70g Butter

1tbsp Lemon juice

1tsp Lemon zest

50g Figs (dried, chopped)

## Method

1. Line a cake pan with butter paper.

2. Sift together flour, baking powder and baking soda. Keep aside.

3. In a mixer blender, put eggs, sugar, butter, lemon juice and lemon rind. Blend till the sugar dissolves and the mixture becomes completely smooth, about 5 minutes.

4. Add the flour mixture and pulse it for 2 – 3 times until combined. Now coat the figs in little flour and add to the batter. Mix a little using a spatula.

5. Transfer it to the cake pan and bake in a preheated oven at 180°C/ 350°F for 45 minute, until a skewer inserted comes out clean.

6. Cool completely before serving.

# Frosting
## & Icings

| Recipes | Vegan | Gluten free | Dairy free |
| --- | --- | --- | --- |
| 1. Chocolate ganache | ✓ | ✓ | ✓ |
| 2. Chocolate rum ganache | ✓ | ✓ | ✓ |
| 3. Cream cheese frosting | | | |
| 4. Lemon glaze | ✓ | ✓ | ✓ |
| 5. Simple buttercream | | ✓ | |
| 6. Cookie and cream frosting | | | |
| 7. Chocolate buttercream | | ✓ | |
| 8. Coconut buttercream | | ✓ | |

# Faults, reasons and remedies

| Faults | Possible reason | Remedy |
|---|---|---|
| Split/ broken ganache | Over mixing | Add about 2 tbsp cream at a time and mix well until it is again smooth and glossy. Add some melted chocolate and mix well.. |
| Buttercream too stiff | Too much icing sugar | Add cream or milk a spoon at a time and mix. Repeat until the desired consistency is reached. |
| Buttercream too soft | No enough icing sugar | Add more sugar, little at a time until you reach the desired consistency. |
| | Kitchen too hot | Refrigerate it for a short period. |
| Lumpy frosting | Icing sugar not sifted | Sifting icing sugar will help to avoid this problem. |

# Common cake frosting mistakes to avoid ——

- **Never frost a warm cake**

  It is tough to resist the urge to ice a cake. But patience is the key to a properly built cake and avoid layers sliding off. I cannot emphasise anything more than cooling a cake completely before frosting. In fact, you can let the cake sit in the refrigerator for a while to make this process even easier. To refrigerate or freeze, wrap individual layers of cake in plastic wrap.

- **Don't slice a cake when it is fresh**

  Dividing cake into layers creates a space for frosting. For this, always start with a cool cake. Refrigerating it overnight is highly recommended. This makes it much easier to ice and stack layers.

- **Don't overbeat the frosting**

  Irrespective of which ever frosting you use, overbeating will lead to a grainy, curdled and unappealing product. So, make sure to whip it only for the required duration.

- **Be careful of the temperature**

  For the buttercream, the butter should be soft enough to hold a thumbprint but not too soft. If too soft, it is very easy to overwork and curdle. After all no one likes a broken and runny buttercream on their cake. If you feel the butter is getting too soft, refrigerate it for a while and re-whip.

# Common cake frosting mistakes to avoid ———

- ## Do not forget to crumb coat

  To keep the top frosting clean and tidy, crumb coating cannot be missed. Simply apply a thin coat of frosting using a pallet knife and chill the cake until the crumb coat is set. This method will seal all the loose crumbs and create a smooth surface for final frosting.

- ## Use proper tools and equipment

  Having a right turn table and pallet knife will make your cake frosting time much easier and enjoyable.

- ## Don't use icing sugar right from the bag

  You shouldn't be missing to sift the icing sugar before adding it to the frosting. This helps to avoid clumps in the frosting and also helps to incorporate extra air giving a smoother and fluffier result.

- ## Don't assume the cake is flat

  A dome typically forms on top of the cake which should be taken off to create a perfectly levelled surface. It needs to be as flat and straight as possible. You can use a ruler whenever you are unsure. Slice any tiny bits that are uneven before frosting.

# Chocolate Ganache

"Chocolate ganache, a heavenly frosting for all the chocolate lovers, is really simple and can be used as a pourable glaze, filling for cakes, truffles and so much more."

Prep: 15 min    Cook: 5 min.    Makes: 300gm    Total: 20 min.

## Ingredients

100g Cream

200g Bittersweet chocolate

30g Butter

A pinch Salt (optional)

———

## Method

1. Heat cream in a microwave safe bowl or in a bowl over double boiler. Remove from heat just before it reaches a boil.

2. Add chopped chocolate, butter and salt (if using unsalted butter).

3. Give it a nice stir and let the chocolate melt completely. Heat in microwave at pulse for 30 seconds or over double boiler if required until completely smooth.

4. Transfer the chocolate ganache to a bowl or jar and cover with a cling wrap or a lid to prevent skin formation.

5. Let it cool and use to frost the cake.

## Variation: Chocolate rum ganache

## Ingredients

1tbsp Rum

## Method

1. Follow the same recipe as chocolate ganache but add rum to it along with chocolate.

## Note

For a vegan and dairy free option, replace dairy cream with a non-dairy cream such as soy based vegan whipping cream. Butter can be substituted by either margarine or coconut oil.

If the ganache becomes too stiff to ice and spread, gently reheat in the micro wave for about 10 seconds and stir well. Repeat until it reaches the desired consistency.

To make white chocolate ganache, simply substitute 400g of white chocolate for every 200g of dark chocolate.

# Cream Cheese Frosting

"Cream cheese frosting goes great on carrot cake, black velvet cake or any other flavored cake too. This recipe makes a nice and stiff frosting, but if needed, sugar can be increased to make the frosting thicker."

Prep: 15 min

Cook:  -

Makes: 300gm

Total: 15 min

## Ingredients

90g Cream cheese

45g Butter

1/4tsp vanilla extract

180g Confectioner's sugar

---

## Method

1. Using an electric mixer, beat the cream cheese and butter together at low speed until completely smooth for 2 minutes.

2. Add in the vanilla extract and confectioner's sugar. Keep beating it. Scrape the sides with a rubber spatula so ensure the mixture is mixed evenly.

3. Keep adding more sugar to the frosting until you get your desired level of sweetness and consistency.

4. Use as desired.

### Note

If you intend to pipe the frosting, sift the icing sugar before adding, as small lumps of sugar can clog the nozzle, especially when using a small tip.

The temperature of the cheese and butter can affect how soft the final frosting is. If it seems too soft, put it in the fridge for about 5 minutes before using.

# Lemon Glaze

" Drizzling a lemon glaze on cakes is an easy way to add a bit of freshness, extra flavor and drama. This easy recipe requires only four ingredients and can be poured over pound cake, lemon fig cake and even cookies."

Prep: 5 min

Cook: 1 min.

Makes: 300g

Total: 6 min.

## Ingredients

300g Confectioner's sugar

1tsp Lemon zest

1tbsp Lemon juice

4tbsp water

## Note

You can flavor this sugar glaze with the addition of any extract you like or a tablespoon of coconut milk powder. You can also dye it with food color of your choice or add in some sugar sprinkles for a funfetti look.

## Method

1. Put confectioner's sugar in a bowl. Add lemon zest and juice to it.

2. Gradually add warm water to it, a spoon at a time and keep mixing until you get the desired consistency.

3. Use it to glaze lemon and fig cake or to dip doughnuts.

# Simple Buttercream

"Simple, creamy and delicious, this buttercream gets ready in a handful of minutes and can enhance the taste of any cake. White chocolate, added in this recipe, takes this frosting to a whole new level."

Prep: 35 min

Cook:  -

Makes: 300g

Total: 35 min

## Ingredients

100g Butter

1/4tsp vanilla extract

150g Confectioner's sugar

50g White chocolate

2tbsp Milk (if required)

____

## Method

1. Using a stand mixer with paddle attachment or a hand mixer, cream butter and vanilla extract together at low speed until completely smooth for 2 minutes.

2. Add in confectioner's sugar and melted white chocolate. Beat for a minute. Scrape the sides with a rubber spatula to ensure the mixture is mixed evenly.

(Adding chocolate would make buttercream more stable and also enhance the favour).

3. Add more sugar to the frosting to make it thicker and sweeter.

4. If too thick, add warm milk; a spoon at a time and if too soft, add more sugar.

5. Let it rest for 20 minutes for the chocolate to harden back.

6. Use as desired.

## Note

Extra buttercream can be frozen for at least a month in an airtight container. The day before you want to use it, let it thaw in refrigerator overnight and then to room temperature before re-whipping it again.

____

## Variation: Cookie and cream frosting

| Ingredients | Method |
|---|---|
| 100g Oreo cookies | 1. Crush the Oreo cookies into powder and add it to simple butter cream. For chunkier texture, keep the cookies chunky. |

### Note:

Don't worry if you end up with a bit less or more crushed Oreos than the recipe calls for- it won't really change the outcome.

## Variation: Chocolate buttercream frosting

| Ingredients | Method |
|---|---|
| 2tbsp Dutch processed cocoa powder<br><br>50g Bittersweet chocolate | 1. Use the same recipe as simple buttercream but add unsweetened cocoa powder along with confectioner's sugar and substitute white chocolate with bittersweet chocolate. |

## Variation: Coconut buttercream frosting

| Ingredients | Method |
|---|---|
| 4tbsp Coconut cream powder<br><br>50g Fresh coconut | 1. Use the same recipe as simple butter cream but add coconut cream powder at step2. Finally add freshly grated coconut to it after it is completely made.<br><br>Note: Use desiccated coconut if fresh is not available. |

# Frozen Desserts

| Recipes | Vegan | Gluten free | Dairy free |
|---|:---:|:---:|:---:|
| 1. Four ingredient mango and mascarpone ice cream | | ✓ | |
| 2. No churn choco-walnut ice cream | | ✓ | |
| 3. Pineapple granita | ✓ | ✓ | ✓ |
| 4. Pistachio kulfi | | ✓ | |
| 5. Vegan Coconut Ice-Cream | ✓ | ✓ | ✓ |

# Four Ingredient Mango and Mascarpone Ice Cream

" This ice-cream is the easiest way to make creamy ice-cream. It takes only a mixer blender and four ingredients to make."

 Prep: 15 min

 Cook: 2 min.

 Serves: 6

 Total: Overnight

## Ingredients

200g Cooking cream

150g Mascarpone cheese

100g Sugar

200g Mango puree

4. Transfer it back to the container. Close the lid and freeze it again.

5. Serve chilled with mango basil sauce.

## Method

1. Heat 50ml cream and sugar till sugar gets dissolved completely. Add this to rest of the cream; also add mango puree and mascarpone cheese. Mix well.

2. Transfer this to an airtight container and freeze it overnight.

3. Now put the frozen cream in a mixer blender jar and blend it till it gets smooth.

## Note

For a twist, you can add cake or fresh mango cut into small cubes or even finely chopped fresh Italian basil after step 3.

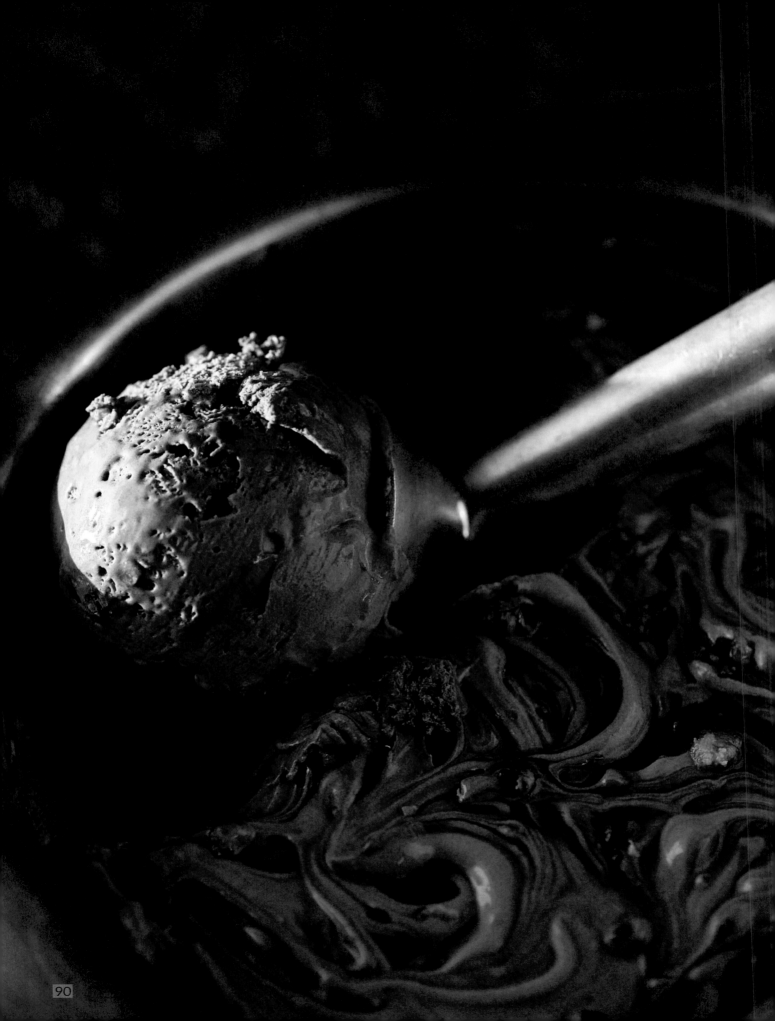

# No Churn Choco Walnut Ice Cream

> " If you crave homemade ice-cream but do not have an ice-cream maker, this no churn ice-cream recipe will leave you spellbound. It is a perfect way to enjoy summer."

Prep: 15 min

Cook: -

Serves: 6

Total: Overnight

## Ingredients

100g Bittersweet chocolate

50g Condensed milk

100ml Milk

3tbsp Dutch processed cocoa powder

150g Whipping cream

1/4tsp vanilla extract

30g Walnuts (chopped)

30g Choco chips

40g Chocolate ganache (refer recipe on pg 76)

A pinch Salt

## Method

1. Using a microwave, melt chocolate in a bowl; add condensed milk, milk and cocoa powder. Mix well.

2. In a large bowl, whip the cream until stiff peak consistency, about 5-6 minutes.

3. Fold the chocolate mixture and vanilla extract into the cream. Also add chopped walnuts and Choco chips.

4. Transfer half of the ice cream to an air tight container, spoon chocolate ganache and add rest of the ice cream. Top with the remaining chocolate ganache and close the lid.

5. Freeze it overnight.

6. Let soften for 2 minutes before scooping.

# Pineapple Granita

" Granita is a frozen Sicilian dessert made from fruit juice until icy. The result is a delightfully crunchy, melt in your mouth fruit ice which can be eaten on its own or served over yoghurt. It can be made with any fruit you like."

 Prep: 15 min

 Cook: 45 min.

 Serves: 6

 Total: 240 min

## Ingredients

500g Pineapple

1tbsp Lemon juice

50g Castor Sugar

1/2tsp Salt

## Method

1. Combine the pineapple, lemon juice, sugar and salt in a blender and blend to a fine puree. Pour it in a container and freeze it for 30 minutes.

2. Take the pan out of the freezer. The puree should have begun to freeze, especially around the edges. Scrape the mixture using a fork and return to the freezer.

3. Repeat this process every 30 minutes for 4-5 hours, until completely frozen and looks flaky.

4. Serve it straight or over whipped cream or yoghurt.

# Pistachio Kulfi

" A traditional Indian ice cream believed to have originated in the 16th century; it is a favourite treat amongst Indians during summers."

 Prep: 15 min
 Cook: 45 min
 Serves: 6
 Total: 300 min

## Ingredients

1l Milk

100g Condensed milk

1tsp Ground cardamom

20g Pistachios

## Method

1. Take milk in a heavy bottom pan.

2. Heat it on simmer, stirring continuously until it is reduced to half.

3. Add condensed milk, ground cardamom and chopped pistachio. Cook it for another 5 minutes.

4. Cool it down to room temperature. Pour into kulfi moulds and place it in the freezer until semi frozen. Put ice cream sticks and let it freeze completely, about 4-5 hours.

5. Serve frozen with more chopped pistachios, if desired.

# Vegan Coconut Ice Cream

" Vegan coconut ice-cream recipe is truly an amazing recipe!
It is creamy, smooth, and rich. It has the perfect ice-cream texture. "

 Prep: 15 min

 Cook: 5 min

 Serves: 6

 Total: Overnight

## Ingredients

200g Whipped cream
(soya based)

35g Vegan coconut
cream powder

140ml Water

50g Granulated sugar

A pinch Salt

2tbsp Corn-starch

50g Tender coconut
(cut into chunks)

## Method

1. Whip the cream to a soft peak consistency. Keep aside.

2. In a medium saucepan, add coconut cream powder, water, sugar, and salt. Bring it to a boil and cook till sugar gets dissolved.

3. Prepare the corn-starch slurry and add it to the coconut mixture and cook till it gets thick. (To check if the mixture is ready, coat a wooden spoon with the mixture and run your finger through it. If the finger leaves a clean mark, it is ready to be used.)

4. Remove it from heat and let it cool completely. Fold it in whipped cream and add tender coconut chunks (if using). Transfer to an airtight container and freeze overnight.

5. Let it soften for 2 minutes before scooping.

# Indian Desserts

| Recipes | Vegan | Gluten free | Dairy free |
|---|---|---|---|
| 1. Mawa | | ✓ | |
| 2. Ajmeri kalakand | | ✓ | |
| 3. Apricot and pistachio roll | | ✓ | |
| 4. Basundi | | ✓ | |
| 5. Chuani | | ✓ | |
| 6. Coconut ladoo | | ✓ | |
| 7. Fried modak | ✓ | | ✓ |
| 8. Gajar ka halwa | | ✓ | |
| 9. Halwa noorani | | | |
| 10. Kala Jamun | | | |
| 11. Malai peda | | ✓ | |
| 12. Pinni | | | |
| 13. Saffron shrikhand | | ✓ | |
| 14. Shahi tukra | | | |
| 15. Sondesh | | ✓ | |
| 16. Thande gulab ki shahi kheer | | ✓ | |

# Mawa

"Mawa, also known as khoya is dried, evaporated milk solids and forms the base of almost every North Indian sweet. It can be stored in deep freezer for up to a month and used to make sweets instantly."

Prep: -

Cook: 95 min

Yield: 400g approx.

Total: 90 min

## Ingredients

2l Milk (full fat)

## Method

1. Take milk in a heavy bottom pan.

2. Heat it on simmer, stirring continuously until it gets thick and lumpy, about 45 minutes.

3. Remove from the heat and let it cool.

4. Use as required.

# Ajmeri Kalakand

" Ajmeri kalakand is a moist, juicy and delicious milk based Rajasthani sweet with delicate, grainy texture. The final look of this sweet is so enticing that it is perfect to be served to your guests."

 Prep: 15 min      Cook: 45 min      Serves: 8      Total: 60 min

## Ingredients

2l Milk

120g Granulated sugar

2tbsp Synthetic vinegar

3tbsp Clarified butter

1/2tsp Ground cardamom

15g Chopped almonds

15g Chopped cashew nuts

15g Chopped pistachio nuts
Silver/gold leaf (optional)

## Method

1. Grease a small aluminium rectangle cake pan with butter and keep aside.

2. Take milk in a heavy bottom pan. Heat it on simmer, stirring continuously until it is reduced to a third, about 30 minutes.

3. Add sugar and vinegar. Let it curdle for 2-3 minutes. Add clarified butter and cook for another 10 minutes stirring constantly till it gets lumpy and turns golden brown.

4. Add ground cardamom and mix well.

5. Transfer it to the prepared tray and flatten the top. Sprinkle some chopped nuts and apply gold/silver leaf (if using).

6. Cut into small rectangles once set. Serve at room temperature.

# Apricot and Pistachio roll

" This dessert is a delectable fudgy sweet, with flavors of pistachio and apricot. Make it for the festivals or any other occasion."

Prep: 15 min

Cook: 15 min

Serves: 8

Total: 60 min

## Ingredients

**Filling:**

30g Granulated sugar

2tbsp Water

50g Turkish apricots (dried, chopped)

100g Pistachio nuts (finely chopped)

**Covering:**

75g Turkish apricots (dried)

150g Mawa (refer recipe on pg 101)

40g Granulated sugar

1/4tsp Ground cardamom

**To garnish:**

Silver (optional)

## Method

1. Stretch and put a piece of cling wrap over the counter and lightly apply oil to it.

**Filling:**

1. Heat sugar, water, apricot and pistachios in a heavy bottom pan until it forms a smooth mixture. Keep stirring until it gets thick and starts to release the sides of the pan. Keep aside.

**Covering:**

1. Using a mixer grinder, blend the apricots until very fine. Keep it aside.

2. Take mawa in a heavy bottom pan and heat it on simmer, stirring continuously until it gets melted again.

3. Add sugar, ground cardamom and the blended apricot. Cook it for another 5 minutes until it get thick and lumpy again.

4. Transfer the mixture over the cling wrap and spread into a 16X4 inch rectangle. Put the filling on one longer end and roll it tightly to get a log. Tie the ends of cling wrap tightly and let it set in refrigerator completely.

5. Once set, remove the cling wrap and cut the roll into 1.5inch long pieces.

6. Serve at room temperature, garnished with silver leaf.

———

# Basundi

"The dessert belonging to Gujarat, Maharashtra and Karnataka is a rich and delicious dessert made using thickened milk, very similar to the North Indian rabri."

Prep: 15 min

Cook: 45 min

Serves: 8

Total: 120 min

## Ingredients

2l Milk

80g Sugar

A few Saffron strands

1/2tsp Ground cardamom

20g Pistachio (sliced)

20g Chironji seeds

**To Garnish:**

Saffron strands

—

## Method

1. Warm 30ml milk and soak saffron in it. Keep it aside.

2. In a heavy bottom pan, heat milk on simmer, stirring continuously until it is reduced to one-third, about an hour.

3. Add sugar, ground cardamom and saffron along with the milk in which it was soaked.

4. Cook it for another 2 minutes and remove from the heat. Add Chironji seeds and sliced pistachios. Let it cool.

5. Refrigerate and serve chilled, garnished with saffron strands.

### Note

Pulp of custard apple can also be added once it cools down to add a unique flavor.

—

# Chuani

"This is a popular Punjabi beverage that has a very rich flavor of gram flour and clarified butter (ghee). Besides being highly delectable, it has a medicinal use as well that benefits in cough and cold."

Prep: 15 min

Cook: 15 min.

Serves: 6

Total: 30 min

## Ingredients

50g Clarified butter

50g Gram flour

1l Milk

60g Sugar

20g Almonds (chopped/slivered)

2. Add a little milk and simultaneously stir to avoid forming any lumps. Mix vigorously to break any lumps, if formed.

3. Add rest of the milk and sugar. Let it come to a boil. Keep stirring constantly.

4. Add chopped almonds and cook for another 5 minutes.

5. Serve hot.

## Method

1. 1. Heat clarified butter in a heavy bottom pan and add gram flour. Cook till it gets aromatic and turns golden brown, about 5 minutes.

### Note:

If ghee is not available, you can cook unsalted butter on low heat until the butter separates and the milk solids rise to the top. Using a spoon, skim the white milk solids on the surface and discard. Now the ghee is ready to be used.

# Coconut Ladoo

" These authentic Indian sweet balls made from coconut, are very tempting to palate which can be made a part of breakfast and evening tea."

 Prep: 15 min

 Cook: 45 min

 Serves: 6

 Total: 300 min

## Ingredients

300g Sugar

60ml Water

200g Desiccated coconut

40g Mawa (refer recipe on pg 101)

40g Condensed milk

A pinch Ground cardamom

20g Cashew nut (chopped)

## Method

1. Add sugar and water to a heavy bottom pan and reduce it to 2 string consistency or soft ball stage.

2. Add desiccated coconut, mawa and condensed milk. Cook till it starts leaving the sides of the pan.

3. Remove from heat and add ground cardamom and chopped cashew nuts.

4. Let it cool down until you can shape it without burning your hands.

5. Divide it into eight portions and make round balls of roughly equal size.

6. Serve at room temperature.

# Fried Modak

"For me, the festival of Ganpati remains the most awaited season of the year because of these delicacies. Modak is considered as one of the favourite dishes of Lord Ganesha and is therefore offered in prayers."

Prep: 40 min.

Cook: 20 min.

Serves: 8

Total: 60 min.

# Ingredients

**Dough:**

250g All-purpose flour

A pinch Salt

2tbsp Clarified butter

2tsp Semolina

Water to knead

**Filling:**

400g Fresh coconut

200g Sugar

1/2tsp Ground cardamom

1tsp Poppy seeds

1l Oil to fry

----

# Method

**Dough:**

1. Knead hard and smooth dough using the mentioned ingredients. Cover and let rest for 20-25 minutes.

**Filling:**

1. Remove the brown skin of the coconut and grate it.

2. In a pan, add grated coconut, sugar, ground cardamom and poppy seeds. Cook till sugar dissolves, about 5 minutes. Keep aside and let it cool.

**Assembly:**

1. Take a small portion from the dough and roll thinly to a disk, about 3 inches in diameter.

2. Add the filling and gather the edges to the center, pinch and twist. Repeat with rest of the material.

3. Deep fry them in medium hot oil till light golden brown. Drain on a kitchen paper.

4. Serve at room temperature.

## Note

Replace clarified ghee with oil for vegan and dairy free option.

----

# Gajar Ka Halwa

" Gajrela as called in Punjabi or gajar ka halwa or carrot halwa is a carrot pudding hailing from the state of Punjab. It is widely eaten during the winter months and Diwali season. There are many instant versions to this dessert using condensed milk or milk powder. But this is a traditional recipe that has been passed down to me by my grandma."

Prep: 20 min

Cook: 120 min

Serves: 8

Total: 140 min

## Ingredients

1.5kg Carrots

100g Clarified butter

1l Milk (full-fat)

250g Sugar

250g Mawa (refer recipe on pg 101)

1/2tsp Ground cardamom

20g Almonds

20g Cashew nuts

20g Pistachios

20g Raisins

———

## Method

1. Peel and grate carrots using a food processor or a hand grater.

2. In a heavy bottomed pot, heat clarified butter and add grated carrot. Sauté for 20-25 minutes.

3. Now add milk. Stir and cook on medium flame until the milk is completely evaporated, about 60 minutes. Keep stirring to prevent burning at the bottom.

5. Once the milk is evaporated and carrots are cooked, add sugar and give it a nice stir. Cook until the halwa thickens, about 20 minutes. Stir every now and then.

6. Add grated mawa and cook for another 10 minutes stirring constantly.

Just before finishing, add ground cardamom.

7. Serve hot garnished with dry fruits and nuts.

———

# Halwa Noorani

" A delicious dessert to prepare when unexpected guests arrive; since it is so quick and easy to prepare. It can enhance the richness of any meal. Though made from common and simple ingredients, it has a very different taste that makes it stand out from all the other halwas.

Prep: 5 min

Cook: 15 min

Serves: 8

Total: 20 min

## Ingredients

400ml Milk (full-fat)

200g Semolina

150g Clarified butter

200g Sugar

50g Nuts of your choice

——

## Method

1. Add milk to a small bowl and soak semolina in it. Keep aside.

2. In a heavy bottom pan over medium flame, heat clarified butter and add sugar. Cook till sugar starts to turn reddish in color, about 5 minutes.

3. Now carefully add the milk and semolina with one hand stirring it constantly with the other. At this stage sugar tends to form lumps but vigorous stirring will dissolve them down.

4. Keep stirring constantly till it starts oozing butter, about 5 minutes.

5. Serve hot garnished with nuts.

## Note

Halwa noorani is a tribute to Mama, my grandma. It was amazing being raised by a grandmother so loving and warm. This halwa was her innovation that truly defined her persona- so royal, so vibrant! This recipe naturally flew to my father and then to me.

# Kala Jamun

"Kala jamun does not need any introduction! It is authentically made with mawa, fried till brown and soaked in rose flavored sugar syrup. No Indian festival is complete without them."

Prep: 60 min

Cook: 30 min

Serves: 8

Total: Overnight

# Ingredients

**Sugar syrup:**

250g Sugar

200ml Water

1tsp Rose water

1/2tsp Ground cardamom

**Kala jamun:**

200g Mawa
(refer recipe on pg 101)

1tbsp Powdered sugar

2tbsp All-purpose flour

1/4tsp Raspberry red powder food color

1l Oil to fry

———

# Method

**Sugar syrup:**

1. In a heavy bottomed deep vessel, add sugar and water. Boil till it reaches '1 string' consistency, about 8 to 10 minutes.

2. Add rose water and ground cardamom. Remove from heat and keep aside.

**Kala Jamun**

1. Take mawa, powdered sugar and flour in a plate. Mash it very well using your hands. There should be no lumps left.

2. Take a small portion of the dough and add red color to it. Knead well until combined.

3. Divide each dough into 42 portions.

4. Take a portion of white dough and gently flatten it. Place a portion of red dough on top, then wrap to seal it completely. Roll into a smooth ball. There should be no cracks. Repeat with rest of the dough.

5. Deep fry them on medium heat till dark brown in color. Strain and immediately add into the sugar syrup.

6. Let them soak overnight.

7. Serve at room temperature.

———

# Malai Peda

" Originated from Mathura, Uttar Pradesh, peda is a semi-soft sweet made of predominantly mawa and sugar. It is traditionally flavored with cardamom, pistachios and saffron. However, flavors like chocolate, butterscotch, rose etc. are really getting popular these days. "

Prep: 15 min

Cook: 20 min

Serves: 8

Total: 45 min

## Ingredients

2tbsp Milk

A few Saffron strands

400g Mawa (refer recipe on pg 101)

30g Sugar

1/2tsp Ground cardamom

20g Pistachio nuts (slivered)

## Method

1. Warm 30ml milk and soak some strands of saffron. Keep it aside.

2. Take mawa in a heavy bottom pan. Heat it on simmer, stirring continuously until it melts.

3. Add sugar, ground cardamom and saffron along with the milk in which it was soaked. Cook it for another 20 minutes until it get thick and lumpy again.

4. Remove from the heat and let it cool till you can handle it with hand.

5. Apply a little oil on your hands. Divide into 15gram balls, flatten a little by hand (a peda mould can also be used) and apply pistachio slivers.

# Pinni

Pinni, a popular Punjabi sweet made using whole wheat flour has a nutty taste and light, crumbly texture. It is a perfect snack during winters as it keeps the body warm."

Prep: 45 min

Cook: 15 min

Serves: 8

Total: 60 min

## Ingredients

125g Clarified butter

250g Whole wheat flour

2tbsp Semolina

125g Mawa (refer recipe on pg 101)

125g Powdered sugar

1/2tsp Dry ground ginger

1/2tsp Ground cardamom

30g Almonds (chopped)

20g Raisins

———

## Method

1. Heat clarified butter in a heavy bottom pan, add flour and semolina. Cook till it gets aromatic and turns golden brown, about 5 minutes.

2. Add mawa and cook for another 5 minutes.

3. Remove the pan from heat. Add powdered sugar, dry ground ginger, ground cardamom, chopped almonds and raisins. Mix well.

4. Let it cool down until warm and can be handled with bare hands easily.

5. Now form into balls, garnish with sliced almonds and let them set completely.

6. Serve at room temperature.

———

# Saffron Shrikhand

“ A very traditional sweet from Maharashtra and Gujarat made with hung curd, flavored with saffron and cardamom.”

 Prep: 120 min.      Cook: 2 min.      Serves: 8      Total: 125 min

## Ingredients

2tbsp Milk

A few Saffron strands

500g Hung curd

140g Sugar (powdered in blender)

1/2tsp Ground cardamom

20g Pistachio nuts (slivered)

## Method

1. Warm milk in a small saucepan and soak saffron in it. Keep aside.

2. Transfer hung curd to a bowl. Add sugar, saffron milk, ground cardamom and mix it using a whisk until smooth.

3. Add pistachio slivers and refrigerate.

4. Serve chilled garnished with pistachio.

# Shahi Tukra

"Conceived and crafted during the Mughal era, the name of this dish means 'Royal Piece.' It is a rich and creamy dessert, perfect to end a royal dinner. It tastes best when the fried bread is warm and the rabri is chilled."

Prep: 15 min

Cook: 45 min

Serves: 6

Total: 60 min

# Ingredients

**Rabri:**

500ml Milk 250g

Mawa (refer recipe on pg 101 )

30g Sugar

1/2tsp Ground cardamom

**Sugar Syrup:**

150g Sugar

150ml Water

1tsp Rose water

6 slices Bread

1l Oil – to fry

30g Chopped nuts

----

# Method

## Rabri

1. Take milk and mawa in a heavy bottom pan.

2. Heat it on simmer, stirring continuously until mawa is completely dissolved.

3. Stir in sugar and ground cardamom. Cook for another 2 - 3 minutes.

4. Remove from heat and let it cool. Chill in refrigerator.

## Sugar syrup

1. In a pan, boil sugar and water to thick syrup. Remove from the heat and add rose water.

## Bread

1. Cut the bread slices into half to form triangles and deep fry in medium hot oil till golden brown in color.

2. Remove on absorbent paper.

## Assembly

1. Take a piece of fried bread and dip it in the sugar syrup. Arrange on a plate and repeat with rest of the pieces.

2. Spoon chilled rabri on top of warm bread and garnish with chopped nuts.

----

# Sondesh

" It is one of the most widely known and appreciated sweets from West Bengal. It is often made for festivals and special occasions, especially Durga Puja."

Prep: 15 min

Cook: 5 min.

Serves: 8

Total: 30 min

## Ingredients

2tbsp Milk

A few Saffron strands

400g Mawa (refer recipe on pg 101)

30g Sugar

1/2tsp Ground cardamom

20g Pistachio nuts (slivered)

## Method

1. Warm 30ml milk and soak some strands of saffron. Keep it aside.

2. Take mawa in a heavy bottom pan. Heat it on simmer, stirring continuously until it melts.

3. Add sugar, ground cardamom and saffron along with the milk in which it was soaked. Cook it for another 20 minutes until it get thick and lumpy again.

4. Remove from the heat and let it cool till you can handle it with hand.

5. Apply a little oil on your hands. Divide into 15gram balls, flatten a little by hand (a peda mould can also be used) and apply pistachio slivers.

# Thande Gulab ki Shahi Kheer

"A new twist to the popular rice pudding made across India. It is a perfect dessert to celebrate any festival."

 Prep: 15 min.

 Cook: 60 min.

 Serves: 8

 Total: 180 min

---

## Ingredients

100g Rice (basmati)

1.5l Milk

100g Condensed milk

1/2tsp Ground cardamom

20g Raisins

20g Almonds (chopped)

20g Cashew nuts (chopped)

60ml Rose syrup

2tbsp Edible rose petals

20g Flaked almonds

## Method

1. Wash the rice and place them in a heavy bottom pan along with milk. Cook gently on simmering for about 45 minutes.

2. Add sugar, condensed milk, ground cardamom, raisins, and nuts. Stir well and cook on simmer until thickened.

3. Remove from heat and let cool. Stir in rose syrup and rose petals.

4. Refrigerate for at least 2-3 hours. Serve chilled garnished with almond slivers and edible rose petals.

# Other Desserts

| Recipes | Vegan | Gluten free | Dairy free |
| --- | --- | --- | --- |
| 1. Chocolate mud pudding | | | |
| 2. Chocolate truffles | ✓ | ✓ | ✓ |
| 3. Classic doughnuts<br>    Filled doughnuts | | | |
| 4. Mango charlotte | | | |
| 5. Pear helene | | ✓ | |
| 6. Pomegranate<br>    cheesecake shooter | | | |
| 7. S'mores hazelnut<br>    fondue | | | |

## Note

This dessert is like an empty canvas with a lot of room for customization. Some of the various toppings are Choco-chips, peanut butter chips, butterscotch chips, crushed candy cane, marshmallows, jelly worms and what not!

# Chocolate Mud Pudding

" This recipe will steal your heart. It is a very crowd friendly recipe making it perfect for any occasion- be it a festival or a get together like Christmas, Easter or Sunday brunch."

Prep: 15 min    Cook: 45 min    Serves: 6    Total: 60 min

## Ingredients

400g Dense bitter eggless cake (refer recipe on page 63)

200ml Hazelnut fudge sauce (refer recipe on pg 157)

100g Chocolate ganache (refer recipe on pg 76)

10g Hazelnuts (chopped)

10g Walnut (chopped)

## Method

Break the dense bitter eggless cake into small chunks and put in an oven safe serving bowl.

2. Pour warm chocolate fudge sauce over the cake pieces. Put dollops of chocolate ganache and chopped nuts on top.

3. Bake at 180°C/ 356°F for 10 minutes.

4. Serve warm on its own or with refrigerator vanilla ice cream and butterscotch sauce (refer recipe on pg 153).

# Chocolate Truffles

"Chocolate truffles are an indulgent chocolate treat made with mainly two ingredients chocolate and cream. They are really easy to make. These small balls can be coated in ingredients of your choice; dip them in milk chocolate or roll them in desiccated coconut or sprinkle some sea salt."

Prep: 45 min

Cook: 5 min

Serves: 6

Total: 50 min

## Ingredients

100g Cooking cream

250g Semisweet chocolate

10g Butter (salted)

50g Dutch processed cocoa powder

---

## Method

1. In a small pan, heat cream and remove before it reaches a boil.

2. Add chopped chocolate and butter. Let it melt completely. Mix well and refrigerate for 15-20 minutes until completely set.

3. Now divide the truffle mixture into 20g portions and form into balls.

4. Roll them into cocoa powder or coating of your choice. Let them sit for an hour to set and get little firm.

### Note

For vegan chocolate truffles, use soy based non-dairy whipped cream and replace butter with a teaspoon of coconut oil.

To make white chocolate truffles, substitute 500g of white chocolate for every 250g of dark chocolate.

---

# Classic Doughnuts

" With the signature bakery taste and texture, these doughnuts are incredibly delicious and indulgent. With this fool-proof recipe, you can make ring doughnuts, filled doughnuts (also known as Berliners) or doughnut holes."

Prep: 100 min

Cook: 15 min

Serves: 6

Total: 115 min

## Ingredients

250g All-purpose flour

1tsp Yeast

25g Sugar

1tsp Vanilla extract

1/2tsp Salt

90ml Milk

20g Butter

Oil to deep-fry

Cinnamon sugar

Melted chocolate

Sugar sprinkles

Lemon glaze (refer recipe on pg 155)

———

## Method

1. Add all-purpose flour, yeast, sugar, vanilla extract and salt to a bowl. Make a well in the center and pour milk in it.

2. Mix well to a smooth dough and turn onto a floured surface. Knead well for about 10 minutes, until smooth and elastic. Add butter and knead for another 2-3 minutes.

3. Place in a bowl, cover with Clingfilm and leave to rise in warm place until doubled in size.

4. On a floured surface, knead for a few minutes, and then divide into two parts. Roll them into 1cm thick sheets and cut using a 2.5 inch doughnut cutter. Place them on a tray lined with parchment paper.

5. Cover with Clingfilm and let them rise till double again.

6. Heat oil to very low temperature and fry them till golden brown from both the sides. Transfer to a wire rack and let cool.

7. Roll in cinnamon sugar or dip in melted chocolate or lemon glaze o any other topping of your choice.

———

# Variation: Filled doughnuts

## Ingredients

**Filling options:**

Whipped cream

Chocolate ganache
(refer recipe on pg 76)

Cream cheese frosting
(refer recipe on pg 79)

## Method

1. Use same recipe as for doughnuts but use a 2.5 inch cookie cutter at step 4 to get a round disk rather than a ring.

2. Proceed with step 6 as for doughnuts.

3. Once cooled, make a small hole on a side and fill your desired filling/ frosting.

4. Dip in chocolate and decorate using sugar sprinkles.

## Note

1. While frying, when you try to lift them, you might create indents with your fingers but once the doughnuts expand with the heat of the oil, they will become plump and beautiful again.

2. If the doughnut cutter is not available, use a 2.5inch cookie cutter and cut the holes in the center using the bottom of a large piping nozzle.

3. The circles of dough obtained at step 4 of the classic doughnut recipe, can be fried (refer step 5 onwards). They are great when dipped in chocolate and topped with sprinkles or simply rolled in cinnamon sugar.

4. Doughnuts usually don't taste the same after a day. However, when dipped in chocolate, the chocolate sets into a crisp shell and seals in the freshness.

## Cinnamon Sugar

Measure 1cup of castor or breakfast sugar into a bowl and add 2tbsp of cinnamon powder.

Whisk together until it is mixed well.

Feel free to decrease or increase the amount of cinnamon as per your taste preference.

# Mango Charlotte

"Mango charlotte is an enchanting dessert with ladyfinger cookie crust and mousse filling adorned with mango chunks on top. Interestingly it requires no cooking, yet its delightful fruity flavor makes it the most liked dish."

Prep: 75 min

Cook: -

Serves: 6

Total: 75 min

# Ingredients

1tsp gelatine

1tbsp water

----

**For the base:**

30g cooking cream

30g castor sugar

60g Mango pulp

**For the mousse:**

180g Whipping cream

**To assemble:**

200g Ladyfingers biscuits

100g Mango (diced)

# Method

### Bloom the gelatine:

1. Add water and gelatine to a microwave safe bowl. Mix well using a spoon and let it rest for 10 minutes or until water is fully absorbed.

### Prepare the base:

1. In a small pan, heat cream and sugar. Remove before it reaches a boil and let the sugar dissolve completely. Add mango pulp.

2. Melt the gelatine at 50% power in a microwave (or use double boiler.) Add this melted gelatine to the base and mix well.

### For mousse:

1. Whip the cream to soft peak consistency.

2. Put a dollop of cream to the base and mix completely. Add the base into the whipped cream and fold to completely mix.

### To assemble:

1. Line a 7 inches round spring form cake pan with aluminium foil.

2. Take the ladyfingers biscuits and place against the sides of the pan snuggly to avoid any gaps. Line rest of the ladyfingers biscuits at the bottom to form a base.

3. Pour the mango mousse inside the mould and let it set completely in the refrigerator.

4. Decorate with mango dices. Refrigerate until completely set.

5. Carefully remove it from the spring form mould before serving.

## Note

For a vegetarian replacement of gelatine, use the equal amount (1tsp)of agar-agar powder in this recipe. To use agar-agar, add it along with the cream and sugar at step 1 of preparing the base and boil the mixture for at least a minute. Boiling agar-agar for at least a minute in the liquid is important to activate its property to set which is not required for gelatine which only needs to be melted.

# Pear Helene

" The ease of preparation and beautiful presentation of this classical French delicacy makes it a stunning dessert for a dinner party."

Prep: 20 min

Cook: 20 min

Serves: 6

Total: 40 min

## Ingredients

6 Pears (peeled, stems intact)

**Syrup:**

300g Sugar

2 whole Cinnamon stick

600ml Water

**To serve:**

6 scoops Refrigerator vanilla
ice cream

350ml Chocolate fudge sauce (refer recipe on pg 157)

## Method

1. Peel the pears and keep aside till the syrup is getting prepared.

2. Combine sugar, cinnamon stick and water in a medium saucepan. Cook over high heat till it reaches a thick consistency and turns golden, around 50 minutes.

3. Add the prepared pears and simmer it for 20 minutes or until cooked but not mushy. Remove from heat and let it cool down completely.

4. Remove the pear from the syrup over a serving plate. Serve with Vanilla ice cream and chocolate sauce.

# Pomegranate cheesecake shooters

" Cheesecake shooters are great for any party. Fun bite-sized treats with such an eye-popping color are guaranteed to be a hit at your next event!

Prep: 15 min     Cook: 20 min     Serves: 8     Total: 45 min

## Ingredients

**Base:**

100g Cookies

40g Butter

**Cheesecake:**

1/2tbsp Gelatine

2tbsp Water

125g Whipped cream

25g Powdered sugar

25g Yoghurt

80g Mascarpone cheese

**Pomegranate jelly:**

100ml Pomegranate juice

20g Sugar

1tsp Agar-agar

**To assemble:**

6tbsp Pomegranate seeds

6no. Mint sprigs

# Method

## Base:

1. In a food processor, add cookies and blend until it resembles breadcrumbs. Add melted butter and blend again for a few seconds. Keep aside.

## Bloom the gelatine:

1. In a microwave safe bowl, add water and gelatine. Mix well using a spoon and let it rest for 10 minutes or until water is fully absorbed.

## Cheesecake:

1. Whip the cream to soft peak consistency and keep aside.

2. In a bowl, take sugar and yoghurt. Mix well until sugar dissolves completely. Add mascarpone cheese and mix well using a hand mixer, about 2 minutes.

3. Melt the gelatine at 50% power in a microwave (or use double boiler).

4. Now add the cheese mixture and gelatine to the whipped cream and fold to mix well.

5. Pour it into a piping bag.

## Pomegranate jelly:

1. Heat pomegranate juice, sugar (omit if using packed juice) and agar-agar over low heat till it reaches a boil.

Let it come down to room temperature.

## To assemble:

1. Take shot glasses and add a spoon of cookie base in each. Press gently using a spoon.

2. Pipe the cheesecake mixture leaving 1cm from the rim. Place the glasses in the refrigerator for an hour, until cheesecake is firm.

3. Top the glasses with jelly and let it set, about 10 minutes.

4. Garnish with pomegranate seeds and mint sprig. Serve cold.

2. Pipe the cheesecake mixture leaving 1cm from the rim. Place the glasses in the refrigerator for an hour, until cheesecake is firm.

3. Top the glasses with jelly and let it set, about 10 minutes.

4. Garnish with pomegranate seeds and mint sprig. Serve cold.

# Note

Pomegranate cheesecake shooters are an easy make-ahead dessert great for masses. Assemble it the day before and refrigerate overnight. Garnish with fresh pomegranate seeds and mint before serving.

If you are do not like the flavor of gelatine, you can replace it with equal amount (1/2tbsp) of agar-agar powder in the recipe. Soak it in 2tbsp of water in a microwave safe bowl and wait for 5 minutes or until it becomes a lump. Heat it in a microwave until it reaches a boil and mix it into the yogurt mixture at step 2 of cheesecake.

# Smores hazelnut fondue

"Delicious and simple chocolate fondue is an easy treat for a family get-together with lots of fun dipping ideas."

Prep: 20 min

Cook: 5 min

Serves: 6

Total: 25 min

## Ingredients

200g Chocolate ganache (refer recipe on pg 76)

200ml Hazelnut fudge sauce (refer recipe on pg 157)

30g Butter

**Dipping treats:**

Bread sticks, cake chunks, cookies, crackers, fresh fruits, marshmallows, mini doughnuts, etc.

## Method

1. Start by preparing all the treats for dipping by putting them on skewers.

2. To make the fondue, combine chocolate ganache, chocolate hazelnut fudge sauce and butter in a bowl and melt it in a microwave or over a double boiler and transfer it to an oven proof serving dish.

3. Arrange mini marshmallows on top of the prepared dip. Bake the mixture on the top rack of the preheated oven at 180°C/ 350°F for 3-4 minutes until the marshmallows get burnt from edges.

4. Serve this warm fondue immediately with crackers and treats of your choice.

## Note:

If you are hosting a crowd for a dinner party, this recipe can be a perfect last minute snack.

Keep it ready before everyone comes. Pop it into the oven for 3-4 minutes and the warm & inviting snack is ready as everyone sits to eat.

# Sauces

| Recipes | Vegan | Gluten free | Dairy free |
|---|:---:|:---:|:---:|
| 1. Butterscotch sauce | ✓ | ✓ | ✓ |
| 2. Caramel pineapple sauce | ✓ | ✓ | ✓ |
| 3. Chocolate fudge sauce Hazelnut Fudge sauce | ✓ | ✓ | ✓ |
| 4. Lemon sauce | ✓ | ✓ | ✓ |
| 5. Mango basil sauce | ✓ | ✓ | ✓ |
| 6. Berries sauce | ✓ | ✓ | ✓ |
| 7. Vanilla sauce | ✓ | ✓ | ✓ |

# Butterscotch Sauce

" Deeply caramel flavored butterscotch sauce is rich, creamy and nutty which makes it a fantastic topping for ice-creams, puddings and cakes."

 Prep: 5 min        Cook: 10 min        Makes: 200ml        Total: 15 min

## Ingredients

150g Sugar

30ml Water

100g Cooking cream

30g butter

## Method

1. In a medium saucepan, add sugar and water. Put it over medium heat and bring it to a simmer, stirring every so often until sugar dissolves.

2. Clean the sides of the pan using a silicone brush dipped in water after every 2- 3 minutes. butter.

3. Cook until it becomes copper color. (If using a candy thermometer, you want it to reach 160°C/ 320°F).

4. Remove it from heat and immediately stir in cream and butter.

5. Mix well and transfer it to a container once it cools down.

### Note

To convert this sauce into a vegan or dairy free recipe, use soy based whipping cream and replace butter with equal amount of margarine.

# Caramel Pineapple Sauce

" It is a rich and buttery sauce with a caramelized fruity flavor. Serve it with cakes, puddings, ice-creams or even cheesecake."

 Prep: 10 min

 Cook: 10 min

 Makes: 200ml

 Total: 20 min

## Ingredients

40g Butter

50g Brown sugar

100g Pineapple (cut into small chunks)

50ml Pineapple juice

A pinch salt

## Method

1. Melt butter in a pan and add brown sugar over medium heat. Stir until sugar dissolves for about 2 minutes.

2. Increase the heat to high. Put in the pineapple chunks and cook till they get golden and are caramelized, about 5 minutes.

Add pineapple juice and cook for another 2 minutes.

3. Remove from heat and add salt.

4. Serve warm with cake, bread pudding, vanilla ice cream, muffins, etc. (It can also be blended into a fine puree if desired).

### Note

This recipe can be made vegan by replacing butter with equal amount of margarine.

# Lemon Sauce

"Lemon sauce is a bright, fresh and vibrant summer sauce which is sweet, tart and tangy. It makes a great topping for puddings, cakes, pancakes and ice creams."

Prep: 5 min    Cook: 5 min    Makes: 200ml    Total: 10 min

## Ingredients

50ml Lemon juice

50ml Orange juice

1tbsp Corn starch

120g Granulated sugar

1tsp Lemon rind

## Method

1. Add lemon juice, orange juice, corn starch, sugar and lemon rind to a pan and cook over medium heat. Stir constantly.

2. Reduce heat to simmer and cook for another 2-3 minutes or until thickened.

3. Remove from the heat and let it cool before transferring to a jar.

4. Serve warm.

## Note

For vegan fudge sauce, use soy based non-dairy whipped cream and replace butter with a teaspoon of coconut oil. If using sweetened whipped cream, avoid adding the sugar given in the recipe.

# Chocolate Fudge Sauce

" This is a great fudge sauce to use for almost any chocolate dessert. It is a snap to prepare with just a few basic ingredients."

 Prep: 5 min     Cook: 5 min     Makes: 200ml     Total: 10 min

## Ingredients

30g Sugar

1tbsp Cocoa powder

75ml Water

75ml Cooking cream

90g Bittersweet chocolate

10g Salted butter

## Method

1. In a stockpot add sugar, cocoa powder, water and cream. Boil for 2-3 minutes.

2. Remove from heat and add chopped chocolate. Stir till completely smooth.

3. Now stir in butter. Let it cool. Store in a jar.

4. Serve warm with ice creams.

## Variation: Hazelnut Fudge Sauce

## Ingredients

2tbsp Hazelnut powder

1/4tsp Hazelnut extract

## Method

1. Follow the same recipe as for chocolate fudge sauce but add powdered hazelnuts and hazelnut extract at step 3.

# Mango Basil Sauce

"With the signature taste of an Indian summer this sauce is a perfect accompaniment to ice creams and sorbets."

 Prep: 10 min

 Cook: 10 min

 Makes: 200ml

 Total: 20 min

## Ingredients

150g Mango pulp

10 leaves Italian basil

20g Sugar

1/2tbsp Corn starch

45ml Water

## Method

1. Heat mango pulp, chopped basil leaves and sugar in a pan till sugar dissolves completely, about 3-4 minutes.

2. Make slurry of corn starch and water in a small bowl.
Add it to the mango mixture and cook for another 2-3 minutes until thickened.

3. Remove from the heat and let it cool down. Serve cold.

# Berries Sauce

"Make this berry sauce with frozen berries stored in the freezer. Use either mixed berries or a single berry as used in this book. It tastes amazing over cheesecake, ice-cream or even yoghurt."

 Prep: 5 min      Cook: 15 min      Makes: 200g      Total: 20 min

## Ingredients

200g Berries of your choice (frozen)

100g Icing sugar

## Method

1. Add berries and icing sugar to a sauce pot. Cook over medium heat for about 5 minutes.

2. Break some berries using a fork.

3. Bring it to a simmer and allow cooking for 5-10 minutes until they become mushy.

4. Remove the pan from heat and let it cool. You may also blend it into a fine puree or leave it chunky.

5. Serve it with ice cream or as a top layer of cheesecake.
This can also be layered in a trifle or as a filling in a Victorian sponge.

# Vanilla Sauce

" A perfect finishing to all kinds of desserts, vanilla sauce is versatile and light. It tastes amazing over pound cake, pancakes and even in coffee.

 Prep: 05 min

 Cook: 15 min

 Makes: 200ml

 Total: 20 min

## Ingredients

50g Sugar

100ml Water

2tbsp Corn starch

30ml Cooking cream

1/2tsp Vanilla extract

A pinch Salt

30g Butter

## Method

1. Bring sugar, water and corn-starch to a boil in a pan over medium heat. Stir in cream, vanilla extract and salt.

2. Cook for another 2 – 3 minutes over low heat until thickened.

Remove from the heat and add butter, stir well.

3. Serve warm or at room temperature over cakes, puddings, sliced fruits or berries.

## Note

Replace dairy based cream with equal amount of soy based vegan whipping cream to make this sauce vegan. If using sweetened whipped cream, reduce the sugar given in the recipe by half (25g). Regular butter can be replaced by the same amount of margarine.

# Recipe Index (A-Z)

# Recipe Index (According to dietary restrictions)

| Vegan | | Gluten Free | | Dairy Free | |
|---|---|---|---|---|---|
| • Mango Basil Sauce | 158 | • Apricot and pistachio roll | 104 | • Chocolate Fudge Sauce | 157 |
| • Berries Sauce | 160 | • Basundi | 106 | • Lemon Sauce | 155 |
| • Vanilla Sauce | 161 | • Coconut Ladoo | 110 | • Mango Basil Sauce | 158 |
| | | • Gajar Ka Halwa | 114 | • Berries Sauce | 160 |
| | | • Mawa | 101 | • Vanilla Sauce | 161 |
| | | • Malai Peda | 120 | | |
| | | • Saffron Shrikhand | 125 | | |
| | | • Sondesh | 128 | | |
| | | • Thande Gulab ki Shahi Kheer | 131 | | |
| | | • Chocolate Truffles | 136 | | |
| | | • Pear Helene | 145 | | |
| | | • Caramel Pineapple Sauce | 154 | | |
| | | • Chocolate Fudge Sauce | 157 | | |
| | | • Lemon Sauce | 155 | | |
| | | • Mango Basil Sauce | 158 | | |
| | | • Berries Sauce | 160 | | |
| | | • Vanilla Sauce | 161 | | |

# Acknowledgement __

Writing this book has been a tumultuous journey with its ups and downs, but a rewarding achievement nonetheless. There are many who have helped me through my journey and I would like to thank them for their efforts.

First among them is my late Grandfather, who has guided me and pushed me to pursue my dreams.

My Papa and my Mom, for their unwavering love and support, and instilling in me a strong sense of discipline.

My brother Guneet, for supporting my creative side through thick and thin, and providing me with valuable feedback at every step.

My friend Aftab, who has been by my side throughout this journey; reading, drafting, and advising.

My friends Shabneez and Madhu, for cheering and pushing me on.

I am immensely grateful to the designer & illustrator (Abha Baxi) and photographers (Niranjan Patwardhan & Sangeet Ahuja) for putting into print this dream.

A special thanks is due to the farmers and producers who provide us with quality ingredients through the fruits of their hard labour, making the recipes in this cookbook possible.

Finally, to all the food enthusiasts and home cooks, who will embark on a culinary adventure through the pages of this book.

To be continued...